Ashton Kutcher

Ashton Kutcher

the
life and loves
of the
King of *Punk'd*

MARC SHAPIRO

POCKET BOOKS
New York   London   Toronto   Sydney

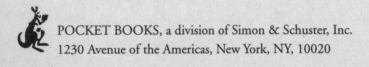POCKET BOOKS, a division of Simon & Schuster, Inc.
1230 Avenue of the Americas, New York, NY, 10020

ISBN: 0-7434-9939-5

First Pocket Books trade paperback edition July 2004

10 9 8 7 6 5 4 3 2 1

POCKET BOOKS and colophon are registered trademarks of
Simon & Schuster, Inc.

Manufactured in the United States of America

For information regarding special discounts for bulk purchases,
please contact Simon & Schuster Special Sales at 1-800-456-6798
or business@simonandschuster.com.

All the People That Count

My wife, Nancy. My daughter, Rachael. My agent, Lori Perkins. Lauren and Megan at Simon & Schuster. Mike Kirby. Steve Ross. Dr. Rozella Knox. The rockers at Poo-Bah. Charles Bukowski. Keri. Chaos. Bad Baby. Dave McDonnell. Tony Timpone. Michael Gingold. Black Sabbath. Cirith Ungol. The Electric Prunes. Cody. Ian. My mom. And finally, to all the people who know the score: This Bud's for you.

Table of Contents

Ashton
Kutcher

Shake Hands with the Devil

L uck? Good genes? A brilliant mind? No. There has to be more to it than that.

Ashton Kutcher must have made a deal with the devil.

The evidence? It's everywhere.

Kutcher was barely out of his bib overalls and life in a one-horse Iowa farming town when he was spotted by a talent scout at a restaurant. She convinced him to enter a local modeling contest. He did. He won. Forget about no pain, no gain. Ashton Kutcher barely batted an eyelash and he was in the winner's circle.

He went to New York, where he promptly won another

contest and was immediately signed to an exclusive modeling contract. Kutcher's long (six feet three), lean (185 pounds), lanky, boyish, Li'l Abner good looks, charming smile, soft piercing eyes, and sense of innocence mixed with a dash of arrogance made him an instant commodity on the catwalks of the world.

After a year of living the high life and making big bucks modeling for the likes of Calvin Klein, Gucci, Versace, and Abercrombie & Fitch, Kutcher decided he wanted to be an actor. The fact that he had not acted since his high school production of *To Kill a Mockingbird* did not seem to faze him. He just knew it was something he wanted to do. Ashton flew to Los Angeles and, on his first day in town, was offered the starring role in two different television pilots. The one he chose was *That '70s Show*.

The show's a hit. Kutcher is an instant star. Playing a bumbling, gullible, not too bright teen Mike Kelso whose sole agenda in life seemed to be to get high and get laid. This is the part he was meant to play. It came so easy to him. Almost too easy.

Shake hands with the devil? Ashton Kutcher must have. How else can you explain what happened next?

Within a year he's signed to a three-picture deal with Miramax. If you blinked you missed most of his early film work. If you didn't, you saw *Dude, Where's My Car?* The critics said he could barely act and wondered—tongue in cheek, of course—if Mike Kelso were the real person and Ashton Kutcher really a figment of our collective imagination. But in the immortal words of Jim Morrison, "the little girls understand" all too well. *Tiger Beat, Teen Vogue, Cosmogirl,* and *Twist* became the media thrones from which Ashton Kutcher looked down on his minions and smiled.

But while the initial marketing of Ashton Kutcher hinged on the preteens and teens accepting his good looks and his favorite color, a tradition that has its roots in the marketing of teen idols all the way back to Fabian, Annette, and, yes, Richard Chamberlain, the brains (that's right, I said brains) behind Ashton Kutcher were already looking toward the bigger picture.

Two years later he's producing and hosting the MTV show *Punk'd*. Playing everyman and bringing the fantasy of real people seeing celebrities get theirs into MTV reality. Less than two years after he uttered his first words in the pilot episode of *That '70s Show,* he's starring in motion pictures that critics hate but make boatloads of money.

Strangely, rather than dismiss him as yet another questionable teen creation who, for the short term, had gotten lucky, the media were beating the drums for him as the consensus next Big Thing. The next year, more production deals, more starring roles, and co-ownership of a hip Hollywood restaurant that is an immediate success. Finally, in 2003, he signs an extension to his *That '70s Show* that adds a reported $5 million to his already substantial fortune.

If it seems like he's never in the same outfit twice, that's because designers from all over the world are lining up to give him clothes in the hopes that he will become a walking billboard. Open his refrigerator and every liquid refreshment is a freebie from a company dying to have him mention their beverage as an integral part of his lifestyle. And the maddening part of it all is that he does not deny the swag; rather Ashton looks upon it as a legitimate perk of his success and tells the suppliers of this graft to keep it coming.

Kutcher has never had a bad hair day—or, for that matter, a bad anything. Don't you just want to smack this guy?

"I know I make it sound easy," Kutcher once said of his rapid rise. "I like it when it sounds easy."

Sound familiar? If you can remember back that far, try Dean Martin on for size. Dean Martin, confidant of Frank Sinatra and Sammy Davis Jr. and an integral part of that late fifties, early sixties institution called the Rat Pack, was never so much an actor as a grown-up little boy who got through the world by playing himself. He was a brash, arrogant, swaggering so-and-so, and, against all the odds, he got away with it. Dino meet Ashton. Ashton meet Dino.

And then there's the ladies.

Kutcher makes no bones about loving women. Unlike 99.9 percent of the men on this planet, however, he has no problem getting the cream of Tinseltown's hottest. He does not appear to put forth much effort. Put him in the middle of a party and, presto, he's a honey-dripping chick magnet. In no particular order, the actor has been involved with or made some kind of time with Brittany Murphy, Ashley Scott, Britney Spears, January Jones, Amy Smart, and Monet Mazur. Currently, the twenty-six-year-old actor is the darling of the gossip columns as the boy toy of the actress Demi Moore, who is fifteen years his senior.

He once partied hard with the underage daughters of the president of the United States right under the noses of the Secret Service, made a play for the wife of his soon-to-be business partner, and, in an extraordinary example of pure balls, walked up to Brad Pitt at a party and asked his permission to take his wife, Jennifer Aniston, out on a date. Pitt just stared at him and reportedly laughed, "Yeah. Okay. Cool." Big mistake on Pitt's part. Ashton took it as tacit approval for him to take his shot, and so, not long afterward, he got onto the set of *Friends* and slipped a note to a wardrobe lady, who gave the note to Jennifer. It read, "What's up with our date?" (She did not respond.)

That Pitt did not deck him on the spot is a further example of the blessing that is Ashton Kutcher's life.

"Women, that's my vice," the actor says matter-of-factly. "I love the company of women."

If Ashton Kutcher's life is not a deal with the devil, I don't know what is.

It's too damned good. The worst thing that's happened to him is that he's had to tell a beautiful woman he was not interested anymore. Or maybe it's the writer's cramp he gets from signing those million-dollar checks. Ashton Kutcher is the guy everybody loves to hate. But the too numerous websites are on fire with hits, the fan mail never stops, and any magazine with his mug on the cover sells out immediately. So why does everybody love this guy so much?

Because at the end of the day, this admittedly business-savvy personality is widely perceived as normal in his approach to life.

Sure he's part-owner in a high-end restaurant, but he's also been known to get excited about the crab leg special at Red Lobster. His taste in cars runs to Land Rover and Chevy El Camino. He's just as comfortable in stylin' P. Diddy duds as he is in a trucker's cap and jeans. And he admits to biting his nails.

The teenager in him can talk your ear off on the relative merits of Van Halen, Prodigy, and White Zombie. When he visits his parents back in the little town of Homestead, he's more likely to be found doing chores for his mother than acting like the Hollywood star he has miraculously become.

His press interviews are less an exercise in prefab answers to softball questions than they are an excuse to hang out and shoot the shit with a complete stranger. He signs autographs. He talks to fans who recognize him on the street. He's been known to pose for a real person's camera. It's rare that Kutcher strays far from his humble blue-collar Iowa roots.

And whether being humble and charismatic is a natural gift or one he's developed as a defense against Hollywood cynicism, it is a talent that has drawn a number of supporters to his side.

"He is just a naturally, really sweet smart guy," said his *That '70s Show* costar Mila Kunis. "He's a really great businessman."

Amy Smart, his costar on the film *The Butterfly Effect,* offered, "He's charismatic, funny, and goofy. He also can become extremely serious and focused. It's an interesting combination."

"He's a real gentleman," said *That '70s Show* costar and good buddy Wilmer Valderrama. "He doesn't kiss and tell."

Kutcher has said that his down-to-earth nature is unique because it's real, which, he has often stated, is contrary to the Hollywood rule of thumb. "People in this town spend too much time working at being normal. I walk through my house that I shouldn't have and get in my car that I shouldn't have and go to my job that I shouldn't have and believe I'm the luckiest guy in the world."

Yeah, but can he act? And is that really important?

Because Ashton Kutcher is a celebrity, not a movie star. And recent history has shown that celebrities only have to look good, not necessarily act well. Is it possible for a celebrity to act? Certainly. Can Ashton Kutcher act?

The jury is still out on that.

In a limited light-comedy, television sitcom sort of way, he can. We're not talking Olivier or Brando. Although with the right material, one can occasionally see a bit of James Dean or Johnny Depp sliding through the perfect pores and smile. But when compared with the collective abilities of the faceless hoards that populate every show on Fox, UPN, and WB, he would certainly grade out at slightly better than average.

As an actor, Ashton Kutcher has yet to prove to anyone that he's more than just a one-trick pony. It would be easy for Kutcher to just ride this lightweight nag to the end and burn out a very young, very rich man. But Kutcher is a smart son of a bitch. In between the rush of expected fluff, he turned in a flawed but interesting dramatic turn in the film *The Butterfly Effect* in early 2004. And even in such abject garbage as *My Boss's Daughter* and such teen gas as *Dude, Where's My Car?* there's been an instinctive, everyman quality that makes up for any great acting chops.

Ashton the actor is not big on the Strasberg Method. He won't talk theory and Stanislavski method acting until your eyes glaze over. He seems to know his place in this universe, and it's actor with a small *a*.

"I don't think you have to be Sean Penn to be a great actor," Kutcher has said, tongue firmly planted in cheek. "But I have no clue what I'm talking about. I've been here for two years, and this is what I've made sense of so far."

Huh?

And ultimately, that may be Ashton Kutcher's saving grace. Like Mike Kelso, the character he plays so well on *That '70s Show,* Ashton seems to wander through life without a discernible clue yet manages to come out smelling like a rose.

Ashton knows that he is perceived as laid-back, moderately talented, not too bright, and awfully damned lucky. And his response to those charges is to be the walking embodiment of the old "sticks and stones" adage. He knows he is not all that and, on more than one occasion, has agreed with his attackers and warned his fans away from something that he does not see as his best work. He has stated on more than one occasion that his ace in the hole is that people have always had such low expectations of him that he is able to use that as an advantage.

Ashton Kutcher is not the consensus all-american. Far from it. You'll find just as many people who despise him and think him the walking butt of a joke as ones who worship the ground he walks on. But let's be honest here. If everybody were madly in love with Ashton Kucher, wouldn't that be kind of boring? The conflict? The tension? We'd have none of that. What makes the world go around is having somebody we love to hate, and Ashton Kutcher is definitely that.

Let's be honest in our assessment of Ashton Kutcher. Most of us would give our eyeteeth to be him, to make his money, to get his action, to have his celebrity. But for most of us that's never going to happen, because we have real lives to live, real dues to pay, and real responsibilities to deal with. So, yeah, a lot of us are just plain jealous.

So why would anybody want to read a book about someone who has made a career out of stumbling into life-changing situations without breaking a sweat or stubbing a toe? Someone a lot of us admittedly don't like. Because Ashton Kutcher, through dumb luck or pop culture's current preoccupation with the likes of Paris Hilton, Jessica Simpson, Anna Nicole Smith, and the Osbournes is as close to living the dream life as most of us will ever get.

Without selling our soul to the devil.

Chapter One

Blue Collar

Grant Wood, the artist of the famous painting *American Gothic*, grew up there. The Quaker Oats and General Foods plants that produce everybody's favorite cereals are located there. Iowa is also the place Herbert Hoover lived the early part of his life.

Beyond those distinctions, Cedar Rapids, Iowa, is blue collar personified. Through the decades, men and women have labored in its factories and its fields. Cedar Rapids children are not raised to be actors and models—or to have a job that requires a shirt and tie. Those that manage to leave its confines never really leave it behind them. The city is in their clothes, it's in their bodies, it's in their souls. Cedar Rapids produces tough men and women who spend their lives for an hourly wage and a weekly paycheck that never quite seems enough.

People like Larry and Diane Kutcher.

Larry Kutcher was born in 1949. The son of a hardworking couple, he was a part of the postwar baby boom that blanketed the United States with a wave of hope and optimism and created families whose traditional values preached an honest day's work for an honest day's pay, church on Sundays, and a salute or hand over heart every time the American flag passed in review. It all sounded right to Larry Kutcher, so he grew to embrace this blue-collar American ideal. Big on sports. Always had a job. Larry Kutcher was somebody who learned to love a part of the country he would never leave.

He grew into a ruggedly handsome man who wore the lines and creases of a working man on his face and hands like badges of honor. In the hardworking community of Cedar Rapids, he was considered quite a catch for any woman.

As was Diane Kutcher for any man. Born in 1952, Diane was smart, self-sufficient, and not afraid to work long hours for blue-collar pay. She was also quite attractive.

That was the first thing Larry Kutcher noticed.

The pair met and fell in love in the early 1970s. Theirs was a courtship that was as formal as it was passionate. They shared the same goals for their lives and believed equally in the importance of family. They married and settled in a small house on the northwest side of Cedar Rapids.

While people in the big cities were setting their lives to the beat of disco and the free-love movement, the Kutchers were strictly nine-to-five people, up with the sun and off to their middle-class, workaday lives.

The factories that produced popular products had long

been a fixture in Cedar Rapids. It's where the vast majority of its citizens punched a clock. For many this was higher education. And it was in these factories where Larry and Diane Kutcher easily found employment.

Larry Kutcher had a job working in a Cedar Rapids butcher shop. When he had the time, he reportedly worked on the assembly line in a Fruit Roll-Ups plant. Diane worked on the Head and Shoulders shampoo assembly line in the nearby Proctor & Gamble factory. It was hard, often dirty, and often tedious work. It brought a paycheck that rarely covered the bare necessities. And though there was a big, wide world out there, the Kutchers felt Cedar Rapids was home and had no desire to see what was beyond the city limits. Theirs was a life built on a simple lifestyle and small pleasures and the hope that they would begin a family in the not too distant future.

Their wish came true when Diane became pregnant and the couple welcomed their first child, a daughter named Tausha, into the world in 1975. Larry and Diane were overjoyed and doted on their firstborn. Since a large family was always in Larry and Diane's plans, it came as no real surprise, early in 1977, that Diane discovered that she was once again pregnant. What came as a happy shock to the Kutchers was the discovery that Diane was carrying twins.

The months leading up to the birth were exciting times for the family. The Kutchers were diligent in monitoring the pregnancy and happily clearing space for the babies that were on the way. Diane Kutcher went into labor on February 7, 1978. Shortly thereafter Christopher Ashton Kutcher came kicking and screaming into the world. Five minutes later, he was joined by his fraternal twin brother, Michael.

The joy of their birth was tempered when it was discovered that Michael had been born with a mild form of cerebral palsy.

Larry Kutcher will always remember that moment. "We were shocked. How could we possibly have one healthy baby and another baby that would be afflicted with cerebral palsy?"

In the first few days after their babies' birth, Larry and Diane felt torn between the reality of twin boys in their lives and the reality that one of them was ill. But they were heartened when told by doctors that though Michael would need constant medication he would live a fairly normal life.

Christopher Ashton Kutcher and his brother grew up in a family that valued togetherness and was big on informality. Although it was never really spoken, the Kutcher family preached a do-your-own-thing philosophy that, from the outset, encouraged individuality and curiosity in their offspring. Of course there were rules to be followed and parents to be obeyed. And if they did not do their chores, they heard about it. But Larry and Diane meted out discipline with a light hand.

Tom McDonald, the high school principal, did not see the results of that parenting for quite a few years but what he eventually saw was the result of a positive upbringing. "Ashton's got wonderful parents," he said. "They would stand up for their child. They raised him well."

The children's parents were big on good-natured teasing and name-calling, so sit-down meals or get-togethers in the Kutcher household often dissolved into aggressive games of verbal attacks in which Christopher learned at an early age to give as good as he got.

"I come from a family where if you do something stupid, you immediately hear about it. So I learned to kind of bring it up first in a funny kind of way before the rest of the family could get you," he recalled.

Christopher also often fell victim to the family's habit of name-calling when he was growing up.

"The big thing in my family was that we were always giving each other nicknames," he said. "I can't remember how many I had as a kid."

Sometimes the horseplay would take the form of stealth attacks from his sister while he was sleeping. "Tausha would always mess with me," recalled Ashton of those early years. "I would fall asleep and wake up in full makeup. Can you imagine how scary that was for a little kid to wake up with lipstick, mascara, and eye shadow on?"

Although fraternal twins, the brothers Kutcher could not be more different in temperment. Michael, due in part to his frail physical condition, was fairly shy and reserved. Christopher, on the other hand, was a much more physical, spirited, outgoing child who made friends easily and, from an early age, seemed to crave the center of attention. Michael would choose his words and thoughts carefully, while Christopher was a shoot-from-the-hip child who could be outrageous even when small.

Ashton maintains to this day that the differences between Michael and himself were the result of chance and nothing more. "We shared the same bedroom and the same influences. With us, everything was always fifty-fifty."

While Christopher would never couch his relationship with his brother in anything but the most positive terms, he would in later years acknowledge that growing up with a twin brother had both its upsides and downsides.

"Your best friend is always with you, and you never have to look for somebody to play with or somebody to talk about stuff with. But at the same time, when you want to be alone, it's very hard to do because there's always somebody there."

Ashton denies to this day that he was a funny kid when he was growing up. However, those in his circle of family and friends noticed a sly streak and a subtle sense of humor that would surface in the heat of verbal combat with family members and friends. Christopher was a quick thinker, one quite capable of formulating smart-aleck comebacks at the drop of a hat.

Ashton was a normal kid, so was prone to mischievous moments that could provoke anger in family and friends. But one look into those innocent eyes and at that childish smile was all that was necessary to smooth things over. Ashton as a very young child had the gift every politician would die for: the ability to make people like him.

The Kutcher family lifestyle revolved around all things physical, and at an early age Christopher was introduced to the wonders of nature and outdoor sports. The young boy soon became adept at fishing, canoeing, and swimming. Michael and he used to spend hours tossing each other around with a wide variety of wrestling holds they learned from watching the pros on television. The boys, by age three, had also developed the annoying pastime of sliding bricks along the top of the family car. At that early stage in his life, every element of Christopher's life seemed to center around rough-and-tumble.

Years later Michael Kutcher, in a bit of understatement, laughingly said, "There was never a dull moment with the Kutcher twins."

Ashton, in addressing the family's outdoors attitude, once jokingly acknowledged that the family never took baths; when they were dirty, they would simply jump in the nearby river to wash up.

His sister Tausha recoiled in horror when she discovered

that Christopher's fascination with the great outdoors and with guns and knives, manifested itself in a favorite pastime, the catching and skinning of snakes and hanging their skins out to dry on a wall. "He was always fascinated by that stuff," she once said.

From an early age, Christopher was taught to face life head-on, so he was often brave to the point of recklessness when it came to competitive, physical things. In team sports he was seldom the biggest, but that did not stop him from competing aggressively against bigger children. It was not uncommon during his formative years for his parents to have to rush him to an emergency room to patch up the results of his missteps in athletic competition or roughhousing with friends. In fact years later, Ashton spent the good part of an interview totaling up the broken bones he sustained as a child. "I broke both arms, a leg, and multiple fingers," he laughingly boasted.

Education was encouraged. College was discussed almost as an afterthought because, although it was never spoken, the unwritten rule was that the Kutcher children, especially Christopher, would follow their parents into the blue-collar working world. It was too early for the children to formulate their life plans, but, as much as a child can reason, Christopher thought working with his hands was a cool thing to do.

To supplement the growing family's income, Larry Kutcher had begun to renovate houses in his spare time. Christopher would accompany his father on many of those jobs; by age seven, he had become adept at scaling high ladders to help his father put shingles on a roof. He was a quick learner, so by all reports by his early teens was quite the all-around carpenter and handyman.

In his personal and professional life, Larry Kutcher was a

go-getter. He was restless when there was nothing to do and would go out of his way to find things to occupy his time. It was a trait that passed easily to Christopher, who in later years acknowledged his father as a major influence in his branching out into many different elements of his professional life.

Christopher was very close to his brother and was fully aware of the physical ailments that often prevented him from joining in on more rough-and-tumble play. In later years, Ashton would often say that he was very proud of his brother and that his triumphs over his physical disability had served as an inspiration to him.

However, the speculation of those around the Kutcher family was that Christopher, while not feeling guilt over his brother's illness, often felt responsible for him. He was always there to step in and defend him and would get scared at any setbacks Michael had and how his brother's illness would affect the rest of the family. Ashton carried this burden with him throughout childhood.

Michael is candid in highlighting the differences between Ashton and himself. "He's always been the good-looking one. He always got the girl. And, when we were growing up, he was always the one who stood up for me."

Joyce Janda Curfman, a former high school classmate of Ashton and Michael, had a front-row seat on what it must have been like. She remembered that Christopher always expressed concern about his brother and that he always "had Mike's back, he protected him. Chris lightened the mood around his brother and took the attention off him."

Even as a young child, Christopher possessed an active fantasy life. Cedar Rapids was far from a cultural, let alone a pop culture center, and so he often took his cues about what the world outside was like through the music that came at him from the radio, MTV, movies, and television programs.

"As a kid, I wanted to be on a television show like *Growing Pains*," he once told an interviewer. "I wanted to be just like Kirk Cameron. For me, that was the pinnacle of an acting career as far as I was concerned. Then I wanted to be on *Saturday Night Live* because that was my favorite show at the time."

Ashton was a sponge, soaking up images of faraway places and fantastic situations, then recycling them into his own interpretation of what the world was like.

At a fairly early age, Christopher became fixated on the idea of California as a fantasyland. "I had this idea of what California was like," he once told an interviewer. "To me, it was beaches and palm trees, warm all the time, and women running around on the sidewalks in bikinis. I had this idea that it was like something out of a Van Halen video."

But while he was a person of some personality and wit, Christopher as a child harbored few fantasies about going off to Hollywood to be a star. Even as a young child, he could not see beyond the streets and farmlands of Cedar Rapids and a life in the factories and the fields.

When they reached school age, Christopher and Michael were enrolled in Garfield Elementary School, which was a mere block and a half from the Kutcher home.

Because of his ailments, Michael wore a hearing aid and very thick glasses. His motor skills were also underdeveloped, which resulted in an ungainly walk. Sadly, all of this made him an easy target for the taunts of his classmates.

Larry Kutcher reflected on this. "The children could be very cruel, and Michael was always being teased about his glasses." But he was heartened that Christopher would always step in and protect his brother from the teasing. The bond between the two brothers had always been strong. Their banding together in the face of the harassment Michael was getting served to cement the bond even tighter.

Christopher's elementary school years were uneventful. By all accounts, he was a better-than-average student who alternated rapt attention to class and teachers with an occasional penchant for misbehavior and acting up. It was all, not surprisingly, good-natured, and nobody felt that Christopher Ashton Kutcher would wind up going down the wrong path. But his parents took no chances.

Christopher was encouraged to become involved in wholesome activities. If there was an organized team sport in town, he would be involved. He often recalls his years in the Cub Scouts and Boy Scouts. He also laughingly explains that there was the added pressure to behave since his mother was the Den Mother and Scoutmaster.

By the sixth grade, Christopher was beginning to express an interest in girls, but, as with most boys his age, it was limited to furtive looks and chaste fantasies of holding hands and kissing. Christopher had his eye on a cute little classmate named Emily. For weeks he had been trying to get up the courage to approach and kiss her. Finally, at a school-sponsored skating party, he took a chance at what was his first romantic kiss.

"We were skating around a roller rink, and I was thinking, 'I'm going to do it. I'm going to do it.' At one point, the lights in the rink went down, it got really dark, and I kissed her. For a while she was my first real girlfriend. But then a month later, she kissed my best friend, and I freaked out, and we broke up."

The end of his elementary school years saw Christopher

beginning to think seriously for the first time about being an actor. But serious for a twelve-year-old still had little in common with reality. The idea of acting looked glamorous and exciting and, yes, sexy on the big and small screen. The dreams were constantly with him. He would imagine himself in the action-packed roles he watched and would create naive fantasies about what it would be like to be an actor and what Hollywood was like.

But with him, too, was the impossibility of having those dreams come true in Cedar Rapids, Iowa.

"If you wanted to act where I was raised, you could either go into community theater or you could find a highly populated sidewalk."

And Christopher did not seem to have the drive or inclination at that point to do either of those things.

The reason was that Christopher was living primarily through fantasy and, if the truth be known, was using that fantasy as a buffer to his growing increasingly restless and bored attitude with small-town life. Christopher was not a creature of habit. He was always looking for the new wrinkle on the old routine. He could get out if he had a plan. But at twelve, he did not know where to begin.

Larry always made a point of treating all of his children equally, and he was quick with a compliment or word of encouragement. But he sensed that Christopher was cut from different cloth from his other two children. Larry felt that his son had a bit of wanderlust in him and, rather than simply tolerate his flights of fancy, he encouraged them to accomplish even the seemingly unreachable goals. "He always had these big ideas, these big dreams. It was like he had places to go."

Christopher took his first tentative steps toward an acting

life the next year when, as a first-year junior high school student, he took to the stage for the first time.

"When I was in junior high, I was too underdeveloped for sports, so I tried out for this play and got such an adrenaline rush when I was on stage."

Christopher's showstopping performance as the Thief in *The Crying Princess and the Golden Goose* garnered laughter, applause, and some heat from fellow students. Not playing sports and participating in activities like school plays was considered an unmasculine pursuit, so for a time Christopher was teased for being less than a real guy. Christopher did not care: He had discovered something onstage that he had never experienced before. Now he knew what it was like to be a rock star.

And the feeling stayed with him for a long time. Whenever anybody asked him what he wanted to be, he would always say, "An actor." When the question was broached in the course of a classroom conversation, his hand would instantly shoot up followed by his stating what he felt would be his future occupation as a movie star.

Of course in a town like Cedar Rapids, Ashton was not taken very seriously. But his parents continued to be supportive, encouraging him to be whatever he wanted to be but privately hoping against hope that their headstrong young son would soon come to his senses and focus on a more sensible life.

Christopher's fantasy world gave way to harsh reality in 1991.

He could sense that his parents were not getting along. The stress of making a living and just getting through each day had slowly ground their love down to nothing. It was also at this time that Larry Kutcher lost his job as a butcher after twenty years, which added further stress to the Kutcher family household.

"When Christopher was thirteen, his mother and I started having differences and our marriage just kind of unfolded."

It was a confusing time for Christopher. He did not want to take sides or get in the middle of anything, so when the words were angry and the tension in the house became too thick, he would just get out of the way and go off into his own world—and into his ever-increasing dreams of being an actor.

"The desire was there ever since I was a little kid," Kutcher would say years later. "I just knew I wanted to be a movie star."

The relationship between Larry and Diane Kutcher continued to unravel, finally reaching a point where Larry moved out of the house. It was a difficult time for them, and it was particularly rough on the Kutcher children.

All the dreams and personal problems within the family were put aside that same year when Michael became very ill. The cerebral palsy had continued to ravage his body throughout the years, resulting in many related health problems and a number of hospital stays. Initially the family thought that Michael had merely come down with the flu. But this time the diagnosis was much worse.

Michael was rushed to the hospital where it was discovered that he had contracted cardiomyopathy, a disorder that weakens the heart muscle. The doctors told Larry and Diane that their son's heart was failing and that to survive he needed a transplant in a matter of hours. Michael was put on an artificial heart machine that kept his heart's normal function going. Then there was what seemed like an interminable wait as doctors attempted to secure an appropriate replacement heart.

Christopher had known insecurity in the early part of his life. But at age thirteen he suddenly felt abject, irrational fear for the first time. He clung to his parents, afraid to let go. His normally happy-go-lucky nature plunged into a deep depression. In a very childlike way, Christopher was ready to make the ultimate sacrifice.

"I was at the point where I wanted to kill myself because I thought he would be able to take my heart," Ashton once said. "When you're in that situation, you'll do anything for that person."

During his hospital stay, Michael recalled, his brother was a constant presence at his bedside. "When I was sick, Ashton never left my side. He showed me the love one brother can have for another."

Finally, at what seemed like the last possible moment, a heart was miraculously found. Michael underwent a harrowing, ultimately successful operation. However, Christopher recalled years later, that was only the beginning of his brother's health scare.

"Things were touch and go for a while. After the transplant, he also picked up a virus, and that nearly carried him off."

In the weeks and months that followed, Michael began to regain his strength. But the stress and strain of the recovery period was the final nail in the coffin for the Kutchers' failing marriage. Shortly after Christopher turned fourteen, his parents filed for divorce.

What scars, if any, were left by the Kutcher divorce are not known. But Christopher would often think about his parents splitting up, and, some speculate, it affected his grown-up relationships.

Happily, there was no rancor in the divorce. In fact the dissolution of the Kutcher marriage was so amicable that when Larry moved out of the Kutcher home, he moved into a home two houses down from the farm. The children were allowed to visit their father anytime they wanted, and, happily, Larry Kutcher continued to be a positive, nurturing influence in their lives. The Kutcher children, especially Christopher, were grateful for that.

Years later he characterized his parents' divorce. "They were so cool. They could not have handled it better."

In looking back on the breakup, Christopher and his siblings realized that they ended up having better, higher-quality relationships with their parents separately than they could ever have imagined. Larry Kutcher was always available with encouragement and words of wisdom. One of the best, Ashton recalled in later years, was "Think with your big head, not with your small head." From his mother, Diane, he would often get input, wisdom, and down-home philosophy.

"I remember when my mother gave me and my friends the sex talk," he once said. "She always taught me to treat women right, to take care of them, and to respect them. I think that was the best advice I ever got."

The Kutcher children had gone through a lot but seemed largely unfazed. Their lives, with obvious differences, went on. But it was also a time for reexamination of their lives and goals. In particular, Christopher seemed to have a lot on his plate.

It was at a time when he had nearly suffered the loss of a sibling and had endured the breakup of his parent's marriage that Christopher made a fateful life decision. Any thoughts of becoming a movie star were cast aside. He would go to college and study biomedical engineering.

So that he could help save the lives of people like his brother.

Chapter Two

The Outsider

Christopher's aspirations to higher education and a career in medicine were taken about as seriously by a lot of people in the town as his acting goals. They figured it was just a childhood fantasy that would eventually give way to the reality of making a living. But Christopher was very serious. For a boy of fourteen, he had done some serious thinking and weighing of options.

"I lived in a tiny town, and I realized that unless I left for California, there wasn't anywhere for me to go with the acting. I couldn't afford to move that far, so I decided to go to school and become a genetic engineer."

Christopher had done a very good job of convincing his

family that his career goals were sincere. "He knew the pain we had gone through with Michael, and he wanted to do something to help other families," said his father.

Christopher was as good as his word in his first year at Washington High School. He maintained good grades while managing to have an active social life and pretty much put the thought of acting out of his mind. Life went on.

Diane began seeing a local construction worker named Mark Portwood. Portwood was an easygoing man, eleven years younger than Diane. They would marry five years later. To Christopher and his siblings, he seemed like a nice-enough guy. In 1994, not long after Christopher had completed his freshman year in high school and had turned fifteen, Diane decided to sell the farm and move the family to the nearby town of Homestead.

Located twenty-five miles south of Cedar Rapids, Homestead, population one hundred, is one of an isolated series of small villages. The town's two-block-long main drag consists of a bar, a post office, and a church. Their nearest neighbor was a quarter mile down the road. The family moved into a small tract house in the middle of a cornfield just off a dirt road.

While the isolation of Homestead did not seem to bother him, the move was tough for Christopher in other ways. In Cedar Rapids, he had developed a large circle of friends, there were familiar places, and he was within walking distance of his father's house. Although Homestead was not too far away, the move for Christopher meant new places, new faces, and a major adjustment to his way of doing things. Making new friends? Now that was a whole other matter.

Compared with Homestead, Cedar Rapids was a big city. And what Christopher quickly found out was that the citizens of Homestead, with their own idea of community and who did or did not belong, did not take kindly to strangers. From the moment the Kutcher family moved there, they were considered outsiders.

Christopher was considered a city kid and, by his own estimation, "a kind of geeky kid." The townsfolk did not care for people from out of town. His early days at Clear Creek Amana High School, which drew students from the surrounding communities and whose entire student population the year Christopher and Michael entered was 230, were a rough introduction to the ways of small-town intolerance. His classmates shunned him, teased him, pushed him around, and made it clear that they did not want him around.

A big problem for Christopher was that his classmates did not take kindly to his always trying to be the center of attention, a trait that instantly rubbed them the wrong way. It also did not help his cause when his outgoing nature branded him as a ladies' man who, according to the school's active rumor mill, was out to steal everybody's girlfriend.

Christopher felt out of place in this new environment but knew that this was now home and he had to make the best of it.

The principal, Tom McDonald, remembered his first impressions of Christopher. "He was a slender, good-looking kind of arrogant young man. He was very certain of himself, and he was very cocky."

Through sheer persistence and his easygoing ways, Christopher eventually carved out a place for himself in Homestead and high school life.

And he did that by getting involved—in everything.

One can look back on Christopher's three years at Clear

Creek Amana High School as a classic case of overachievement. He joined the choir and the science club. Despite the continued impression that acting was for sissies, he joined the school's Thespian Society, where he enthusiastically threw himself into each production.

He appeared in the school's productions of *Rumors, Little Shop of Horrors, The Curious Savage, More Than Meets the Eye,* and *To Kill a Mockingbird.* It was clear from the moment Christopher stepped on stage that he really loved what he was doing and that he had a passion for acting.

"During his years he participated in a number of plays," said McDonald. "The first couple of years, he was playing primarily support roles. He was all set to take on lead roles, but, as I recall, every time he was set to take the lead in a play, he would get into trouble."

Though he was still slight of build, Christopher was active in the woefully undermanned school sports program, participating in track, wrestling, and football. His grades continued to be outstanding, resulting in his making the National Honor Society his entire stay at Amana.

McDonald once described Christopher "as a brilliant student."

Much has been made of Christopher's supposed lackadaisical attitude toward high school, and it is claimed that his good academic standing was more of a fluke than anything else. The reality was that Christopher was a voracious reader whose habits ran the gamut from popular fiction to the classics like *The Great Gatsby.* McDonald recalled that Christopher was an "A student with the occasional B."

"He was a very good student," he continued. "We don't have honors classes at the school, but I recall Christopher's taking the most challenging curriculum. He took advanced

chemistry, advanced math, including calculus and trigonome-
try, and advanced English classes."

By his admission, Ashton later looked back on his high
school years as important to him for dealing with feelings of
uneasiness.

"I always had feelings of insecurity in high school," he
said in an interview. "The possibility of failure was always
with me. But just about everything I learned in high school
has come in handy. I know a lot of my positive work ethic
came about because of high school."

Christopher's ability to fit into all groups and social strata
came easy to him. He sensed that by fitting in and getting
along he would be able to survive in what he had perceived as
a closed and cliquish environment. And he did. The kids who
had pushed him around and taunted him quickly became his
good friends.

McDonald had a firsthand look at how Christopher went
from outsider to one of the popular students. He recognized
a clear method in the way Christopher eased into every possible segment of school life.

"He made friends rather easily," he recalled. "He was
streetwise. He knew how to play the system. He could sweet-
talk a teacher or even myself. He would joke with you. But he
knew how to get what he wanted."

As tough as it was on Christopher, Michael had it
rougher, so Christopher would go out of his way to introduce
his brother around and make him feel welcome. If he sensed
that his brother was being picked on, he would step into the
middle and crack some joke or do something to lighten
things up to put the attention on him rather than his brother.

It was during his sophomore year of high school that
Christopher lost his virginity. To this day, Ashton, ever the

gentleman, refuses to name the girl. However, he does offer that it happened in the Iowa woods, that he hardly knew the girl, and that it was over almost before it started.

Although the consensus was that Christopher was an outgoing person who made friends easily, years later he looked back on high school with different memories.

"When I was in high school, I had one really close friend. Everybody else was coming and going and doing their own thing. As I came to be a senior, I had more friends and more acquaintances, and I started to get to know more people."

In his high school days he was not what one would consider a ladykiller. "I didn't have a date to homecoming my freshman year," he recently confessed. "I didn't have a girlfriend until I was a sophomore in high school. I was a pretty late bloomer. The girls weren't really going crazy for me. They had better options."

But as his social awkwardness melted away and he began to expand his circle of friends, Christopher also discovered a wild side that he had not known he had. And he contributes a big part of his turn to the isolation of Homestead.

"There's less to do when you're in the middle of nowhere," he once said. "There wasn't even a drive-in movie. So you had to use your imagination to keep yourself busy or to keep yourself from getting into trouble. It was pretty much one of those communities where you had to make your own entertainment. In an environment like that, you get pretty creative when it comes to having fun."

Christopher did his best throughout his high school years to avoid trouble. He worked a variety of really odd jobs. For a time he skinned deer at a local butcher shop. He also spent time sweeping up Cheerios dust at the local General Foods plant (a job that carried over into his college years). When money became particularly tight, Christopher was also known to sell his blood.

He and a small group of friends would often hunt in the surrounding woods or go snowmobiling. He would often take to the road, racing motorcycles or his friend's Oldsmobile Cutlass up and down what passed for city streets. On the weekends, he and his buddies would go to Cedar Rapids to watch the monster truck shows or go dirt-car racing in the fields that surrounded the village.

Occasionally he would be overzealous in his fun and would be pulled over by the local police for his high-speed antics. In a town like Homestead, it was not long before everybody knew Christopher had been busted.

"The worst thing was that everybody in my town had a police scanner, and for kicks they'd sit around and listen to who was getting into trouble. My parents knew if I'd been caught speeding before I even walked through the door. We'd go to the cornfield with a keg of beer to party and the cops would already be there waiting for us."

"He never really did anything too far out of the ordinary," remembered his principal. "He had a couple of minor run-ins with the law. But nothing exceptional. Even when he got into trouble, he was still a likeable kid."

However there were those times when the party animal in Christopher would come out. Parties in Homestead often consisted of a keg of beer in the middle of a cornfield where, he recalled, "I would just get hammered." He has admitted on several occasions to having smoked marijuana and years later would regale reporters with stories of getting high in his basement while listening to Prodigy and White Zombie albums and staring vacantly at black light posters. However, in his first two years in Homestead, his radical outbursts were kept fairly under the radar, thanks in large part to the school's Thespian Society.

Because the reality was that, while outwardly he was determined to stay the course and become a biomedical engineer, inwardly his promise was steadily losing the battle to the side that craved the spotlight. And with good reason. In such productions as *To Kill a Mockingbird,* Christopher was showing a considerable, if raw, talent. He had a deft hand with dramatic roles, and when it came to comic portrayals, it was a short leap from his basic personality that added depth and no small amount of laughs.

And after years of teasing, Christopher was slowly gaining a modicum of grudging respect from his peers. Christopher was on the horns of a dilemma. He wanted to act in the worst way. He was also feeling a growing need to get away from this small-town life and see what the rest of the world was all about.

Going into his senior year of high school, Christopher had no idea which side would win.

As it turned out, the ultimate winner was his first real love.

Christopher fell in love with Abbey McDonald the first time he laid eyes on her. She was beautiful. She was smart. Abbey was also the principal's stepdaughter. And Christopher had a reputation, while far from the worst in town, as being a hellraiser. Abbey was interested in Christopher and flattered by his attention. But she said no to his asking her out for a date.

"She was definitely my first love," recalled Ashton. "I worked really hard to go out with her. I sent her flowers and everything. Finally she said yes."

Things could not have been going better for Christopher

at this point. He was young and in love, and he had just been offered the plumb role of Daddy Warbucks in the school production of *Annie*. Christopher was so psyched at getting the part that he willingly shaved his head to conform to the look of the character. Christopher was on top of the world.

But one night, in a moment of extremely bad judgment, Christopher and a friend decided to sneak onto the high school campus in the middle of the night and get drunk. The pair were discovered reeking of beer in the boys' bathroom by the local authorities. In a town like Homestead, Christopher's indiscretion immediately branded him as Public Enemy No. 1. Christopher's parents were called to the principal's office for a meeting. While the other boy was also punished, Christopher's punishment was the worst possible thing they could have done to him.

Christopher was dropped from the play.

He was apologetic, realizing that he had not only lost points with his girlfriend and, by association, her father but that there would be hell to pay at school. However, in large part because of his good academic standing, he was allowed to stay in school. But, as his father recalled, some damage had been done.

"He was devastated," recalled Larry in an interview. "He changed as an individual. He became very bitter toward the school for what they had done to him. It was like he didn't care what happened after that."

Despite his feelings, Christopher managed to remain on his best behavior for a while. Then, near the end of his senior year, he once again got into trouble.

After a pleasant evening with his girlfriend and her stepfather, in which Christopher and Abbey watched movies in the family room in the basement while McDonald and his wife watched television upstairs, Christopher was politely told by

McDonald at 12:30 A.M. that it was time to go home. Christopher left, then met up with his cousin, who was in trouble. He had an important test coming up, a test he had not bothered to study for. A plan was instantly hatched.

Christopher and his cousin sneaked back into the high school on a mission to steal a copy of the test. It was later reported that while on campus, the two boys also broke into a number of vending machines and took the money out first. Then Christopher used his skills with tools to pick the lock in a matter of seconds, and the pair went into the school's main building. Unfortunately, the pair did not know that they had triggered a silent alarm in the school library.

McDonald recalled that "they had tripped a silent alarm that led right into the local sheriff's department. The sheriff's deputies came out and surrounded the school building."

The moment they came out of the building, Christopher and his cousin were arrested, handcuffed, and put in the back of a patrol car. McDonald had been notified of the burglary attempt and went to the school. Where he saw that it was Christopher who had been arrested, he was not pleased.

"When I saw him handcuffed in the back of the patrol car, I was so mad that I would have killed him if I had gotten to him. That's how upset I was."

Christopher expected his parents to bail him out. His mother had other ideas. "He was upset," recalled Diane, "but I made sure that I didn't pick him up until the next day to teach him a lesson."

The response from his stepfather was even more direct.

"My stepdad told me if I ever got thrown in jail, he would let me stay there for the night," Ashton related years later. "So I called him and said, 'Hey, I'm in jail.' And he said, 'Have a good night,' and he hung up the phone."

Christopher spent the night in jail. He later recalled that it was not a pleasant experience. He was dressed in a regulation prison jumpsuit and spent most of the night listening to other prisoners protest their innocence. When Ashton was released the next morning, he had learned his lesson.

He was ultimately charged with third-degree burglary, and was found guilty in a court trial, and was sentenced to 180 hours of community service and put on three-years' probation. His cousin was similarly punished, but that was not the worst part for Ashton.

Abbey and her stepfather were shocked and disappointed by his actions. Although they eventually forgave him, Abbey broke up with him and ended up going to the senior prom with somebody else. As part of his punishment, Ashton was deprived of all his school clubs and sports for six months.

"We have a very strict conduct code here," said McDonald. "What Ashton did was as grievous a violation against the school as anybody could have committed. And it was his second major violation. It was not my choice but rather it was the student code of conduct that we followed."

Christopher was crushed. He spent his final days in high school saddened and embarrassed by the consequences of his actions because in a town like Homestead, everybody knew what happened and nobody would ever let him forget it.

Academically, Christopher had continued to excel. As a senior he enrolled as a nonmatriculating student in the University of Iowa's post secondary education option program, which allowed exceptional high school students to take one university level class per semester while still in high school. This small step outside of Homestead agreed with Christopher, who reportedly did well in the PSEO program.

Diane Kutcher and Mark Portwood made their long-term

relationship official when they married in 1996. Christopher Ashton Kutcher marched in his graduation ceremony that same year. Christopher accepted his diploma with mixed emotions, because he knew a big part of his life was about to change forever. Some of his longtime friends were going off to college. A lot of them were following in the footsteps of their parents and going off to jobs in the factories or on the farms. Christopher was only mildly nostalgic for the good times. He was ready for the world outside of Homestead and whatever that part of his journey would bring.

But while the future for his mother and stepfather looked bright, Christopher felt he was at an emotional crossroads. He was confused, unsure, insecure.

And he did not know which way to turn.

Chapter Three

On the Catwalk

The urge to act was as strong as it had ever been, so much so that Christopher was secretly planning elaborate escape fantasies in which he would go out to Hollywood and become a star. However the desire to make his family proud and, indirectly, to keep the promise he made at the time of Michael's illness proved even stronger.

There was also the matter of the burglary conviction that continued to hang over his head and, with higher education, to limit his options. By the terms of his probation, Christopher was not able to leave Iowa. Which meant that Hollywood was not possible in his immediate future.

So shortly after graduation and a summer spent weighing

his emotions and options, a reluctant Christopher Ashton Kutcher packed his bags and moved down the road to the University of Iowa, where he enrolled as a freshman with the dual majors of chemical engineering and biochemistry in August 1996.

"Those were two very difficult majors," said Larry Lockwood, the university registrar. "And the classes were hard to get into. So I think that tells you something about that student."

During his freshman year, Christopher adjusted well to college life. He studied hard, soaked up the complex medical and scientific knowledge like a sponge, and joined the campus fraternity Delta Chi. Christopher was like any young man away from his parents and his home town for the first time: He marveled at the newfound freedom and was serious about his now adult responsibilities. On the surface, things seemed to be going according to his well-thought-out life plan.

But beneath the surface, Christopher was in pain.

"I wasn't doing it for me," he confessed years later. "I was doing it for my family."

Christopher's conflict was nothing new. For generations, children had been faced with the choice of doing what they wanted or doing what they felt was right. Christopher, despite his childhood adherence to college and a medical career, was classically torn, by a constant battle between his reality and his dreams.

His state of mind resulted in Christopher leading a sort of Jekyll-Hyde existence throughout his freshman year at college. By day he was the diligent student who knew his way around medical compounds and scientific equations. To teachers and fellow students, he seemed destined to make good on his goal of getting into medicine.

By night he was in a self-destructive spiral.

He would party hard with his Delta Chi buddies at parties that seemed a ready option almost every night of the week in and around the University of Iowa. To his fellow students, Ashton was the good-time party guy. What few had an inkling of was that the young man was most likely attempting to salve his fears and insecurities with alcohol and drugs.

"I thought I knew everything, but I didn't have a clue," Ashton recalled years later. "I was smoking a lot of weed and partying. I woke up many mornings not knowing what I had done the night before. I played way too hard."

Amazingly, this lifestyle did not seem to interfere with his staying focused on his studies during the day. While his grades through that first year have never been made public, what is known is that they were good enough for Ashton to stay academically off probation through that first year.

Christopher continued to work part-time jobs to supplement his meager student loan money. It was more of the same dead-end, blue-collar jobs that had driven him to escape to a better life, and it was a reminder of what could happen to him if he failed at college and lost the opportunity for a better life. When he visited home, Christopher did a good job of hiding his true feelings and frustrations. If either his mother or stepfather sensed something was troubling him, they said nothing, hoping that he would make the right decisions and, most important, to do what would make him happy.

Christopher returned to the University of Iowa for his first-year finals in even more turmoil. In his mind, he had fully decided that he wanted to go to Hollywood and be a star. Any guilt he felt at going back on his word had long since faded into the background. The idea of sitting down and taking final exams in preparation for an occupation he had lost all passion for put him in a state of panic. But his in-bred drive to succeed resulted in his passing his finals and getting As in all his classes, except in calculus, where he barely scraped by with a D.

But how bad had things gotten for Christopher in those dark days at the University of Iowa?

"I was lying in my dorm room one night, and my roommate was having sex with his girlfriend," he painfully remembered. "I didn't have a girlfriend. I was failing a class. I was miserable."

He felt he could not continue to handle the rigors of life at the University of Iowa, that he was only fooling himself, and that he had to get out and try his luck in Hollywood. The arrival of a student loan check for $800 appeared to give him the way out.

"I packed up everything I had into a duffel bag. I didn't have a car, so I decided I was going to walk to the airport, buy a ticket, and leave."

Darkness settled in on the campus. It was time to go.

True to his word, Christopher sneaked out of his frat house at 2 A.M. on an Iowa morning and began the twenty-mile walk to the airport. It was cold and it was a long walk. But Christopher was determined that his life was about to change for the better.

"I was convinced I was going to do it. I got about ten miles, decided to forget about it, stuffed the bag under a bush, and walked to my mom's house. She took me to get my bag, and I went back to college the next day. That was my halfhearted attempt to get out of Iowa."

But while halfhearted, it was an attempt that he continued to beat himself up about. He would question his courage at the failed attempt. He would ask himself how much he wanted to be an actor and just how badly he wanted it. The dreams of stardom were still a fantasy. If only he could find a way to make them a reality.

Christopher completed his finals and returned to the University of Iowa for his sophomore year in May 1997. But his passion for the medical world was now all but gone. He sleepwalked through his classes, getting passable marks and not really caring. The extracurricular partying continued at a brisk pace. He continued to use alcohol and marijuana. Christopher did not like what he was becoming.

He knew in his heart this was not what he should be doing nor what he wanted to do. He also knew that he could not drop out of college and return to Homestead and a life in the factories. To do that would be to admit failure. And he was not ready to do that. Christopher's future was completely unsettled. If he were to make his fantasy come true, he was going to need to be pushed into action. So he continued to bide his time and wait for a sign that it was time for his life to change.

One night midway through his sophomore year, Christopher was taking a study break at a nearby campus restaurant, when a local woman named Mary Clarke walked past him. She took one look at him, stopped dead in her tracks, turned around, and walked back to where he was sitting. Christopher was amused at this strange woman who was looking him up and down and was embarrassed by what he perceived as her forwardness. He was not ready for what happened next.

Mary introduced herself as a local talent agent and asked Christopher if he had ever thought about being a model. Christopher did a double take and laughed. Obviously he had not.

"I didn't even know that guys did that," he later recalled of that incident. "I didn't even know that was a real job. I thought Fabio was the only real male model. Then I realized, 'Oh, the Marlboro Man isn't really a cowboy.'"

The woman went on to explain that she was scouting for a local modeling competition called the Fresh Faces of Iowa and that they were looking for contestants. Christopher thought about it for a minute.

"I knew I didn't look like what I thought a model was. I didn't look like Fabio. I always felt I was kind of awkward. I just didn't see myself in that light."

Ashton took all those self doubts into consideration and was ready to pass on the offer when the talent scout said the one thing that could possibly have changed his mind. She told him that modeling would be a good step toward a career in acting.

Ashton was on board.

The contest took place at a local shopping mall. The regulations for even a small regional contest like Fresh Faces of Iowa were an eye-opening experience for Christopher. In a sense, his naïveté actually was to his advantage, for while other, more seasoned models nervously fixed themselves in a mirror or tugged and tucked at their clothes and hair, Christopher just did what came naturally to him, which was to smile and look relaxed in front of the judges and during the various competitions.

What almost certainly helped him in this early competition was that he was far removed from the group of high school friends who would have teased him for even considering modeling. Free from their razzing, Ashton, perhaps for the first time, was free to be himself.

"It seemed pretty simple," he said of that first competition. "All I had to do was walk from where I was standing to a spot, turn around, and walk back again."

Christopher figured somebody else would win. After all, how could somebody who did not have a clue about what he was doing capture the top prize?

So no one was more surprised than Christopher when the judges announced that he had won the 1997 Fresh Faces of Iowa contest. Surprise turned to excitement when he discovered that first prize was the opportunity to travel to New York and participate in the International Modeling and Talent Convention, a meat market, in essence, in which models compete in various competitions, meet with agents, and possibly sign with prestigious modeling agencies.

Christopher was up for it, sensing that this might be the push he needed for a shot at stardom. If nothing else, it would get him out of Iowa for the first time in his life. His mother and stepfather gave him somewhat reluctant encouragement, perhaps sensing that whatever this trip to New York did for Christopher would be what he really wanted. His probation officer said that the short trip out of state was okay as long as he continued to report to him. Christopher was on his way.

Christopher was like a kid in a candy store as he walked the streets of New York, taking in the sights, staring at the shabbily and sharply dressed people, and seeing more people on one block at rush hour than populated the entire town of Homestead. He called home, excited at just being in the big city.

"He said, 'This is great! You should see these buildings,' " his sister Tausha recalled in an interview. "I think it was a big deal for him to be doing something on a bigger level than being in Iowa."

The modeling competition in New York was much like the Fresh Faces of Iowa competition, only magnified a thousand times. Hundreds of perfect-looking men and women walking the catwalks and competing for the opportunity of a professional modeling contract. Christopher was excited, his adrenaline was pumping. But he managed to project the same down-home innocence that had gotten him to New York in the first place.

"I've never seen agents, collectively, go 'Oh, my gosh!'" recalled Clarke. "He had this quality, a star quality. That's what they saw."

Christopher's poise and middle-American ways impressed a number of talent agents who were trolling the convention looking for new talent. One agent was so impressed with his striking good looks and down-home attitude that she immediately rang up a talent manager she knew and strongly suggested that she have a meeting with Christopher.

Stephanie Simon had been in management a long time, so nothing or nobody who crossed her path in the modeling business could surprise her. She trusted the talent agent who reported this find but she would ultimately decide for herself. Christopher, on the other hand, was blown away at the opportunity to meet with a high-powered manager. He was so excited that his having nothing formal to wear did not keep him from walking through Simon's door on the day of the meeting.

"He came in to see me, and he had overalls on," Simon related in an interview. "But the second I met him, I just knew. I knew he was going to be huge. I told him on the spot, 'You're moving to New York.'"

Christopher was excited and just as quickly pragmatic. It was easy to justify his jumping at the chance. His education, or rather his attitude toward it, was all but dead. He half-heartedly felt that he could always go back later. Right now he was anxious to embrace this wonderful new world that was being offered to him on a silver platter.

He immediately called his parents and told them in no uncertain terms that he was now a model and that he would not be returning to school. "They were like, 'Go for it!' " he said of their response.

Enthusiasm aside, Christopher's parents' response was, understandably, typically Midwestern. They warned him not to get crazy and to be practical in his business dealings. In their hearts they knew their son had made the right decision. The next call was to his probation officer, who, after a lengthy discussion, bent the rules just enough so that Christopher could leave the Iowa jurisdiction for an extended period of time and move to New York.

Simon immediately signed him to the prestigious Next Agency. She also suggested that there were already so many models in New York with the name Christopher that it might be in his best interest if he changed his first name. Christopher chose to just bump his middle name up to his first name, and thus, late in 1997, Ashton Kutcher was born.

Though the name had been shortened, his middle-American ways were still very much in evidence. It soon became apparent to those around him that Ashton was still pretty much a babe in the woods in New York City. He was not pushy, aggressive, or arrogant. Naive? Yes? But friendly in that small-town way that has proved so endearing.

He related to strangers as well as to people he knew in an outgoing, aw-shucks manner that often had people poking fun at him. But there was also something refreshing in the way that Ashton interacted with people and responded to situations that drew even the most sophisticated and worldly people in the modeling world to him.

Ashton was a charmer who, while not overtly competitive, could get on your good side and, more often than not, into situations that would benefit him. This was very much the Ashton Kutcher of Homestead, Iowa, whose sincerity and innocence continued to serve him well by allowing him to ease himself into the tough, very competitive world of modeling.

One of the first to befriend Ashton was the model Tom Welling. They met on a shoot and immediately became fast friends. Their paths crossed throughout the years, eventually in Hollywood.

Once Ashton had signed on the bottom line, Simon took over his care and feeding. To cut down on expenses, she moved the aspiring model in with her brother. She got him his first passport and advised him on the audition process and how important it was to look and act the part of a model even before he landed his first job. Consequently, the first major undertaking for Ashton was to go shopping.

For Ashton, learning the modeling ropes was like starting first grade over again. He knew nothing about how models presented themselves to potential employers, what the work entailed, or how much he would be paid, so he would often chuckle at the things his manager would tell him. But ultimately he knew what he was being told was important, and so he was grateful for the help. "She's my lifeline," he later said of Simon. "Without her I don't survive."

Ashton was already going to auditions and learning the craft of modeling on the job. By all accounts, Ashton proved a natural at photo shoots and runway shows. He was photogenic, projected a sense of believable innocence, and seemed a universal perfect fit for almost anything he was asked to model. For a raw rookie, Ashton was far from hesitant; even in early auditions, he came across as confident and poised.

But for Ashton, modeling was anything but an overnight success. Despite the backing of the Next Agency, Ashton worked only sporadically in his first days and weeks as a professional model. He was learning the fine art of attending multiple calls in a day and experiencing the frustration of not landing a job at any of them. But rather than get down, Ashton embraced each rejection as part and parcel of the learning curve in the modeling world.

Ashton was gradually becoming comfortable in this world. This was where he belonged.

Modeling was serious business, a three-ring circus of egos, money, and big business that had chewed up and spit out countless players in this high-stakes game. But Ashton had chosen to sidestep those notions of money and celebrity. At this early juncture, it was all just a lot of fun and games to Ashton. He was modeling clothes, running all over town in a seemingly endless hustle to find work. When he did land a job, he was paid more money in a day than he had ever seen in the jobs he held in Iowa.

It was during a photo shoot for an Abercrombie & Fitch catalog that Ashton became acquainted with January Jones, a fellow model and an aspiring actress. There was an instant attraction between the pair. She was from South Dakota, a state that, much like Iowa, embraced a traditional, blue-collar ethic. Like Ashton, she was a model who had designs on an acting career. January also came across as sweet, kind, and innocent. These were qualities that had always appealed to Ashton in the fairer sex. But what proved a big attraction to Ashton and one that entered into all of his relationships was that she was somewhat more experienced in the real world, and so he could learn from her. The latter appeal, no doubt, was left over from the strong influence his mother had on his life.

At first look, it seemed like a love match made in heaven. But neither Ashton or January at that point seemed ready for a relationship. But they were both young and alone in the big city for the first time. They were ready for friendship, so they bonded instantly.

Ashton and January would get together for meals, go off to auditions together, or just hang out doing nothing when they were in town. Those in their circle, however, sensed that if nothing romantic was going on then, it was only a matter of time. The reality was that both were too busy in their own lives to consider romance as an option.

After a few local jobs and his first professional acting job in a Pizza Hut commercial that, for whatever reason, never aired, Ashton, as more of a lark than anything else, agreed to appear in a short film entitled *The Distance* directed by a film student at New York University.

Ashton's first experience in front of a camera was an eye-opening one. Before, he could only imagine what being in front of a camera would be like. What he found was the unglamourous process of numerous takes, flubbed lines, and the importance of hitting his mark. Rather than bored, Ashton was excited by the reality of filmmaking, and it once again brought to mind fantasies of acting and the Hollywood life.

But for now there was this strange new reality of modeling to deal with. Even though Ashton was working fairly regularly, he was still not making a lot of money. Instant soup became a staple in the young model's diet. But even at his poorest, Ashton would not cry out for help.

"It was my starving-model stage," he joked years later.

"But there was no way I was going to quit or call home for money. That was not an option."

What he did do was borrow money from friends and his manager. Never enough to get deeply in debt and always with the promise that he would pay it back.

Ashton was soon whisked off to Europe for several months of modeling assignments and auditions, but only after checking with his probation officer for a final time to make sure it was okay for him to leave the country. For somebody who had never left Iowa and was barely getting used to the hustle and bustle of New York, the idea of winging across the Atlantic and experiencing Europe for the first time was almost too good to be true for Ashton.

Once he landed on the continent, Ashton discovered that the difference between modeling in the United States and Europe was as different as night and day.

"The whole modeling situation is different in Europe," he recalled. "In New York you can be a model and pretty much be left alone. But the attitude toward models is different over there. Models are recognized by people on the street. I remember one day, we were in Venice, shooting on the Piazza San Marco and this crowd of what seemed like hundreds of people gathered to watch us work. When we had finished the shoot, the crowd broke into applause."

What he would discover was a reality he had not expected but that he enthusiastically embraced. He had gotten a taste of the modeling life in New York—the endless auditions, the long hours of work when there was work, the constant fear of rejection, and the all-night parties that were considered a major networking requirement for models on the way up.

But during his time abroad, he would come to discover the European modeling scene to be all that and more. "You travel around the world for free. You live out of your suitcase and you have all the freedom in the world."

Ashton's excitement was most certainly tempered by homesickness. He was on the phone to his parents at least once a week to let them know what he was doing and, more important, that he was all right. He also checked in with January from time to time. Ashton missed home, but he was also having the time of his life.

Ashton's European odyssey took him to the modeling runways of Milan, Paris, and London, where he was often walking the catwalks wearing such megabrand names as Versace, Gucci, and Calvin Klein. The young model quickly got into a manic routine that had him typically sleeping six hours a night and going to as many as twenty auditions in a single day, in which he would often have fewer than five minutes to convince the casting agent that he was the right body for a particular show.

He did not know any language but English but his boyish charm and his willingness to experience everything quickly made him one of the hottest models working the runways overseas. His attitude also made him many fast friends among fellow models who could sense that, while competitive, he would never stab them in the back for the sake of a job.

Ashton remembered one particularly hectic week in Milan when he worked the runways for nineteen shows for clientele as diverse as Gucci, Versace, and Dolce & Gabana. He laughingly recalled that, during the stay, he and his fellow models would literally run through Milan on a daily basis just to get to the next audition or next show on time. And it was during those frantic days on the catwalk circuit that Ashton learned much about the audition process that would aid him in later years.

"When you're a model you have five minutes to make an impression on someone," he once told an interviewer. "They look at what you look like first but, after that, no one wants to work with an asshole. So you basically have five minutes to say to them, 'Hi, I'm not an asshole.' "

Ashton proved particularly adept at projecting a cooperative image, so he worked a lot. In fact his modeling career was taking him all over the world. On one particularly grueling leg, he found himself in Chicago for two days, New York for a week, Milan for two weeks, Paris for two weeks, London for a week, New York for a day, Chile for a couple of days, then back to New York and Chicago. Initially, he had kept his room in his manager's brother's apartment in New York, but he was there so rarely that, almost without thinking, on his stopovers in New York, he would inevitably end up knocking on his good friend January Jones's apartment door.

Ashton's presence in the apartment fueled a friendship that quite naturally evolved into love. The comfort level the pair had with each other was obvious. That they were both in the same business and could understand the emotional ups and downs and the periods they would often be apart was a major consideration.

"Yeah, it's tough but we survive," he once said of their long periods of time apart. "I miss her, but what are you going to do? She has her job, and I have mine."

It was the emotional and moral similarities that cemented their romance. January was much like his vision of the small-town girl he most likely would have married if he had stayed in Homestead. January has never really been forthcoming on what attracted her to Ashton, but it's a safe bet that a lot of it had to do with his bright smile, easygoing ways, and the sense of comfort she experienced around him.

In a typical case of tongue-in-cheek understatement, Ashton once described their budding romance by saying, "I asked if I could crash at her pad, and basically I never left."

Ashton's education in the way the modeling world worked continued. An admitted party guy who had no problems staying up all night after a show, Ashton was nevertheless able to avoid the problems of drugs, alcohol, wild egos, and even wilder sex that often travel in tandem with runway models. Whether it was his small-town morals coming to the fore or his commitment to his budding relationship with January, Ashton managed to avoid the pitfalls of the catwalk. He did admit in later years that he saw a lot of his fellow models succumb to temptation and that it was his ability to "know my limits" and be "strong-willed" that kept him from following suit.

It also did not hurt that Ashton was not taking his job too seriously.

"To be perfectly honest, modeling is a very silly way to make a living," he said recently in looking back on those wild and crazy days. "It's the least important job in the world. All you are is a coat hanger for other people's creations. I didn't take it all that seriously. I was not one of those people who got up first thing in the morning, looked in a mirror, and wondered how good I looked."

One way Ashton was able to keep everything in balance was to get out of the big cities on his rare days off and go to the small villages or explore the countryside of whatever country he happened to be in. It was during those moments that his small-town roots would show and he would revel in the simple life that was now so far removed from what his life had become. As somebody who grew up working with his hands, Ashton could often be found in the stalls and marketplaces of small villages, finding much to admire in the artistry and craftsmanship of the people. He also appreciated the old-world sensibilities that contrasted with the hustle and bustle of big-city life.

"I loved Rome," he once said. "After visiting Rome, I kind of fell in love with the place. The history of the place was just incredible."

One of the most humbling experiences Ashton experienced while a model took place shortly after he signed an exclusive modeling agreement with Gucci. One day entailed modeling a wide variety of clothes, including different styles of thong underwear in front of then Gucci designer Tom Ford.

"There I was, stark naked and trying on a lot of thongs in front of the chief executive of Gucci who was gay," recalled Ashton. "It didn't mean a thing. I didn't care then and I don't care now."

There were no openly gay people where Ashton came from, but he felt at ease modeling in front of Ford. He would later observe that all the Gucci head seemed to be interested in was the clothes and not the models.

Although he had left the life of Homestead behind, Ashton would occasionally return to visit his parents and friends and to work off one element of his probation.

"Part of his sentencing for the burglary was that he had to come back to the high school and serve as a volunteer tutor," recalled McDonald. "We set him up in the nurse's office and, during his breaks from modeling, he would come back here and help the kids. Chris was a very intelligent kid. Whatever subject a kid might be having trouble with, he was sharp enough to help them."

What Ashton discovered on those trips home was that the people of Homestead barely had an inkling of what he was doing. But that did not stop them from teasing Ashton about modeling being a sissy occupation that no real man would do.

"I don't think there was a lot of knowledge of just what it was he was doing," remembered McDonald. "I was more familiar than most because of his relationship with Abbey, and I would see him in *GQ* catalogs and things of that nature. But I don't think many people really had much knowledge about what he was doing."

Well into 1998, Ashton had hit his stride as a model. He was taking on only the biggest paying jobs (reportedly as much as $5,000 a day) and living a life he only dreamed about a year before. But while by modeling standards, he still had many more profitable years ahead of him, the desire to act was burning brighter than ever. Whether it was his naïveté or the confidence of being young and successful in the middle of a fantasy lifestyle, Ashton was convinced that he should, without any formal training, be setting his sights on Hollywood.

He regularly spoke to his manager about getting him some acting jobs. Stephanie Simon had heard Ashton's pleas more than once. Every model had illusions of being an actor at one time or another. Few ultimately have the chops or temperament to make the transition. But there was something in Ashton that made her think that he might just be the one to make it. From the beginning, she felt he could be an actor. And so, as his modeling career took off, behind the scenes she began making the calls and calling in favors that gave Ashton Kutcher his shot.

His first shot at a major motion picture came when he was offered the opportunity to audition for the lead in *Varsity Blues*. Not surprisingly, Ashton was broke, since despite being well paid, most of his money went to management, clothes, and other expenses. He had to borrow money for the subway to the audition. Ashton was good but not good enough and lost the part to James Van Der Beek.

One day, during a couple of days off in New York, Ashton got a call saying he should hop a plane immediately and head for Los Angeles. It was TV pilot season in Hollywood, and Simon was sure she had the perfect opportunity for Ashton.

Something called *Adventures in Chemistry.*

Adventures in Chemistry was reportedly a comedy that featured a character not unlike Ashton, a bit naive with a good heart. Even though the character was like him he did not feel that it would work, but realistically, at this stage in his career he had to take the chance. He was the new kid on the block. Most actors would kill to be in the position to even have a shot at it, so he put his personal feelings aside and got on a plane going west.

Pilot season is the ultimate Hollywood crapshoot. Each year hundreds of ideas for new television shows are floated. Some get to the point where a script is commissioned (called a pilot), a few get to the casting stage, fewer still actually get made, and even fewer still make it to the fall television schedule. That even fewer new shows make it through a full season before being canceled is almost an afterthought.

At least it was to Ashton as his plane touched down at the Los Angeles airport.

Simon had done her best to explain to Ashton what pilots were and how they often turned into regular series and what the audition process would be like, but it went right over his head. In his own quite logical but totally naive frame of reference, why would anybody go through all the trouble to make something they don't intend to keep on the air?

Besides, this was the first time Ashton had been to Los Angeles. From the moment his plane began its descent until he pulled up in front of his hotel, his head was on a swivel, taking in all the sights and sounds of Los Angeles and the fabled city of Hollywood. To his way of thinking, the dream had finally come through. He had arrived.

The place where *Adventures in Chemistry* and other pilots were being cast was an exercise in controlled chaos. Agents, managers, and casting agents went in and out of rooms. Actors sat in nervous clusters in hallways, studying their audition script pages or fixing their hair and makeup. To Ashton, this was very much like what he experienced every day as a model. Although he tried hard to hide it, he was as nervous as the rest as he awaited his call to audition for the pilot.

Ashton Kutcher failed his first audition in Hollywood. Until recently, he had never gone public with his reasons, so one could only speculate that the nervousness, the lack of acting experience, his not being the right type, or any combination of the three had something to do with it. Nowadays, the actor has no problem dissecting that first Hollywood misstep.

"I went in, did the test, and the material just was not funny."

Ashton was on his way out the door when he met another casting agent on the hunt for actors for his pilot.

"I was walking out of the building, and this guy stops me and says, 'I want you to come in and read this.' "

So rather than hopping a plane back to New York, the aspiring actor ended up auditioning for another pilot.

It was for a cowboy-surfer dramatic series called *Wind on Water* that was considered a sure thing for the coming television season because the actress Bo Derek (*10*) had already agreed to star in it. Although leery of the concept, Ashton went in and nailed the audition. His performance was so strong that the producers immediately offered him the role.

"They told me that we would be going to Hawaii to shoot the pilot and that everything was going to be great. All I could say was, 'Whoa!' "

Ashton was thrilled to have landed the part even though he felt the concept was a little far-fetched. He didn't see himself as a cowboy or a surfer. So it was almost as an afterthought that he took his manager's advice and went across the street for yet another audition she had managed to get him while he was auditioning for the *Wind on Water* people. This other pilot, a comic look at a 1970s group of teenagers, was called *Teenage Wasteland*.

The show, also known in its early development as *The Kids Are Alright*, was much like the period comedy *Happy Days* except that it takes place in 1976 and would have more emphasis on sex and drugs. There were the rebellious teenagers, the token nerd, the clueless party girls, and the all-too-understanding parents. The character sketch presented to Ashton with his script pages was that of a gullible, not very bright high school student with a heart of gold.

Ashton also found much to like in the show's emphasis on a small town where bored teenagers struggled to find something to do. "With the show, you actually believe you are living in the most boring town on the face of the earth," he once said. "I kind of grew up in that situation so I'm able to relate to my character on the show."

That the character of Mike Kelso seemed a mirror image of Ashton's real life was obviously more coincidence than design. Ashton, at least at that moment, did not see the connection and did not take offense at the idea he might be playing a comic caricature of himself. He just went for it.

Those privy to the audition were universal in their praise. They confirmed that Ashton instinctively had a level of raw, instinctive comedic talents that one rarely finds in a younger actor. By the end of the audition, the producers and casting people were laughing themselves silly, which in Hollywood is always a good sign.

The producer, Bonnie Turner, recalled that what really knocked them out that day was the way Ashton looked. "But he got the role because everyone else was reading the character as stupid, but Ashton made him naive."

That may well have been the producer's perception. However, the reality was that Ashton, without a discernible acting background and a small-town, wear-your-emotions-on-your-sleeve attitude, was doing nothing more than being himself.

"I just knew I nailed it," he recalled of the audition. "I look a lot like Kelso, and I have the same energy."

He was in and out of the audition in under thirty minutes. That was all the time needed for the producers of the show and the representatives of Twentieth Century Fox Television to agree that Ashton was their man. Upon receiving the news, he was elated.

Moments later he realized that he had already agreed to play the part in *Wind on Water.*

Ashton was not aware of the enviable position fate had cast his way. Through sheer luck, he was going to end the day employed. The consensus was that *Wind on Water,* with Bo Derek's involvement, would most certainly wind up on the fall television schedule. *Teenage Wasteland* was considered a long shot at best. Logic dictated that Ashton go with the sure thing.

Teenage Wasteland was the show Ashton really wanted, but

he was not about to commit potential career suicide by blowing off one before he had the other. So he went to the producers of *Teenage Wasteland* and told them that he already had a quasi-commitment to *Wind on Water*. If he did not get a firm offer by 4 P.M., he would have to go with the other show. Ashton spent a restless afternoon waiting to hear from the *Teenage Wasteland* people. Finally, at 3:45 P.M., they came back with an offer he could not refuse.

Ashton went back across the street to the *Wind on Water* people and told them he had changed his mind and was going with the sitcom instead. The producers were visibly upset and did their best to change his mind, reminding him that *Wind on Water* was going to be on NBC and that *Teenage Wasteland,* if it did get picked up, would be on the much smaller Fox network. Ashton wavered. Then the producers hit Ashton where it hurt.

"They told me that I had already auditioned for a comedy [*Adventures in Chemistry*] and that I had not been good at it. I felt like they were trying to tell me that I was not right for comedy. That's all they needed to say. I went with the comedy."

Ashton Kutcher, meet Mike Kelso.

To say that luck entered into Ashton's getting the *That '70s Show* role is an understatement. With limited acting skills and only his gut instinct to go on, he had landed on his feet in a series that ultimately lasted a long time. In one twist of fate, Ashton had instant security, instant fame, and a break that most actors work their entire lives for but never get. In the classic sense, Ashton Kutcher was about to become that oddity, a real live overnight success.

Ashton was overjoyed. He called January to tell her the good news, and they immediately made plans for her to give up her apartment in New York and join him in Los Angeles. He called his parents who were likewise thrilled for him but also a little concerned about how their innocent son would make out in a Hollywood they had heard so many horrible stories about. Eventually he got around to contacting his parole officer to tell him that he would now be residing in Los Angeles.

For his part, Ashton continued to project that innocence and friendliness of small-town America to his new circle of Hollywood friends. Again he was gently, often openly, mocked by his contemporaries for his Homestead ways. Many thought it was an act and a very good one at that. However, they eventually came around to realize that he was not affecting this personality. Ashton really was this wide-eyed innocent. It was a personality they liked and eventually gravitated to.

Ashton was sky-high as he set about readying himself for his first acting role. He discovered that one of the requirements for playing a period comedy was that he would have to look the part, which meant wearing his hair a bit longer than he was used to. He was not crazy about the idea but felt that learning to use a blow-dryer was a small price to pay for stardom.

Adding to his preparation for the show was research that required him to listen to seventies music, such as Abba and Kiss, to get in that seventies frame of mind, to look at old high school year books and TV commercials, and, yes, even talk to his parents to get a working idea of what the seventies were like. Ashton was alternately amused and bewildered at what he discovered about that bygone era.

"That was creepy," he related two years after the show's premiere. "Everything was so raw and primitive. It was almost scary."

Shortly before the cameras were set to roll for the pilot episode, *Teenage Wasteland* became *That '70s Show.* Not too long after the name change, Ashton and the other cast members, Topher Grace, Laura Prepon, Danny Masterson, Mila Kunis, Wilmer Valderrama, Kurtwood Smith, and Debra Jo Rupp, sat around a long table at the studio where the pilot would be shot. For the first time they did a cold read of the script. Ashton felt a bit insecure at his reading but chalked it up to first-day jitters and the fact that many of his castmates had more experience than he did.

That '70s Show's pilot finally went before the cameras.

And for Ashton, things only got worse.

"The first day we were going over the script and shooting the pilot, I was petrified," he painfully recalled. "The first time we did a read-through, I didn't know what was going on. I had a pencil in my hand, and I was so nervous that I snapped it. I was so scared."

To be fair, Ashton was not alone in his first-day jitters. For many in the cast, this was likewise their first big opportunity. A lot was riding on the pilot. A successful television series could easily run seven years and open up their careers to unimaginable opportunities. A regular paycheck would also be nice.

But to Ashton the others seemed more poised and comfortable in their surroundings while he was seemingly more awkward and unsure. Ashton had always dreamed about what acting would be like. In his fantasies it was always easy. That acting was really hard work and required a certain degree of talent had never entered into his dreams. His fantasies had not prepared him for days like this.

So Ashton took those first days of filming very hard. He imagined that every move he made was the wrong one, that his timing was totally off, and that the lines he had to say, while funny on the script page, fell dead when he said them. Outwardly, Ashton was still high on the excitement of being in Hollywood and on the verge of becoming a star. Inside he was scared and unsettled, insecure in his performance, and, perhaps, in the thinking that had led him to this point.

After all the years of dreaming and hoping, Ashton had finally made it to the magic kingdom. But now he was having second thoughts.

Chapter Four

Dude, Where's My Career?

Ashton's insecurities had manifested themselves in the form of a stilted, stiff, and, worst of all, forced performance in the pilot. His outgoing personality had suddenly frozen into broad and obvious caricature in front of the camera.

This was the first time he had to deal with insecurity in his professional life. Ashton was not sure how to do it.

However, his shortcomings in those early days of filming were more than overcome by the show's funny premise and the ease with which the ensemble cast, including Ashton, worked together. One look at the pilot was all that was necessary for the Fox network to pick up *That '70s Show* for the 1998 fall season.

Ashton was assured by everyone around him that he had done just fine and shouldn't worry. But as the first five episodes of *That '70s Show* came and went, Ashton could see no improvement in his performance, and behind the scenes concern was expressed by others that the promise he had shown in the audition had all but disappeared. Ashton thought he had been terrible during the first episodes of *That '70s Show* and spent many a sleepless night fearing that he was about to be fired.

"I just kept doing stupid little things," he painfully recalled. "Things that I knew I wouldn't normally be doing in a million years."

One day during rehearsals, the producer-writer Bonnie Turner took Ashton aside.

"I was convinced I was about to be fired," he recalled. "She explained that there's a trick to doing comedy, that it was like a waltz. She taught me that to do comedy, you don't need to try and be funny."

Ashton took her advice, and the result was immediate. He appeared more natural at the roundtable readings for each script, and, during filming, he was more comfortable with the nuances of the script and the comic beats required in a television sitcom. His was not an overnight transformation, but the consensus was that Ashton was slowly and surely rounding into shape as a workmanlike comic actor.

The producers were particularly impressed with the way he had molded the character of Mike Kelso in something of flesh and blood rather than the typical sitcom caricature. The actor had, perhaps subconsciously, began to incorporate more of himself into the role, which, at least according to the producers, seemed to fit the character of Kelso just fine.

"He's an extremely intelligent individual," said his castmate, Danny Masterson. "He's a smart guy who happens to be very good at playing dumb. You can't be that stupid if you studied biochemical engineering in college."

January joined Ashton in Hollywood, and the couple soon found a two-story apartment in a secluded section of the Hollywood hills. In the coming weeks they spent a lot of time making their apartment into a home.

The romantic spark between Ashton and January was still burning hot. January had always been guarded about her feelings for Ashton, although she would occasionally slip into gushing praise of his physical beauty, phrases like "He's very beautiful, almost womanly." For Ashton, whose true feelings always seemed to be worn on his sleeve, his feelings for January ran deep.

"I enjoy having a companion through all this stuff. She appreciates the things I do for her, and she takes care of me. We respect each other's space and our work. And I think what keeps it going is that we're such good friends. If we get in a fight, we'll hate each other for a day, but then the next day, we'll fall in love all over again."

It all sounded too good to be true. What kind of relationship it was remained vague. Reportedly, marriage was never discussed, but neither did they ever express the desire to see other people. They were seemingly quite happy at that point to live together and see what developed.

That '70s Show got off to a so-so start. The comparisons to *Happy Days* were often mentioned, as were the heavy doses of lowbrow humor with their emphasis on sex and drugs. On the upside, critics liked the chemistry between the cast members and felt the show was the perfect vehicle for its perceived target, the teen audience. Ratings for the first half of the season were good if not spectacular. One thing was becoming

quickly clear. Not too surprisingly, Ashton immediately in-
gratiated himself with the rest of the cast. He could charm
them with his good looks and innocence, display a biting
sense of humor with a double entendre joke, and, during
breaks in filming, be the life of the party as he plucked out
songs on a guitar.

Based on the amount of fan mail and audience response,
Mike Kelso had become the breakout character on the show
and *That '70s Show*'s resident sex symbol.

Not that Ashton was really into that sort of praise. He was
levelheaded about that sort of thing, preferring to focus on
the more tangible parts of being an actor. Which meant work
and little else.

By this time, the actor had settled into a fairly predictable
routine. He had instantly bonded with his fellow cast members, especially Danny Masterson and Wilmer Valderrama,
and it was the rare time when various cast groupings were not
out doing something together or hanging out at somebody's
home.

Ashton was not one to forget his old friends and continued
to travel back to Homestead to hang out with his buddies from
high school and, most important, be with his family.

"When I go home, I still do chores around the house," he
said of his frequent trips home. "I usually try to make it back
for Christmas, Thanksgiving, and Mother's Day. I like going
back because my family is really cool."

And the way the townsfolk treated him now was much
different. Gone was a lot of the sarcasm and teasing that had
been part and parcel of his modeling days. To his friends,
being on television was a much loftier goal. In their eyes,
Ashton was no longer a sissy boy; he was now a television
star.

"I have all the same friends," he once said of his aversion to getting caught up in success. "I just have a better job."

But the reality was that when not reading the show's script for the coming week or hanging out with January or his friends, Ashton was already preparing to take his career to the next level. He was smart enough to realize that with success came stereotyping, and while he enjoyed comedy and the character of Mike Kelso, he looked to the diverse roles of people like Tom Cruise as a blueprint for the kind of career he wanted to have.

"I definitely don't want to be stuck in the 'pretty boy' category," he said early in his career, "because that means you'll only get parts as a romantic lead, and I want to go beyond that. I want to be a great character actor."

Not long after relocating to Hollywood, Ashton hooked up with Jason Goldberg, who became his de facto manager and business partner. Goldberg got a firsthand look at Ashton's charisma the night he met the young actor at a birthday party he had thrown for his wife, the actress Soleil Moon Fry (the grown-up "Punky Brewster"). After introductions, Goldberg watched in amazement as Ashton began to hit on her. He was amazed at the sheer audacity and arrogance of the actor, but the manager in him knew instinctively that somebody with those traits could go far.

Through informal meetings, Goldberg discovered that Ashton, beneath the shy-country-boy demeanor, was a workaholic with an entrepreneurial spirit. Going into the end of the first season, it was obvious that not only was *That '70s Show* going to be around for a good long run but that Mike Kelso was going to be an integral part of it, if not the driving force behind the show.

Ashton and Jason were not about to pull a David Caruso

(the actor who left *NYPD Blue* for a film career that never materialized), nor were they going to make unseemly demands for more pay. But they did have some ideas on where they wanted Ashton's career to go.

The pair agreed that they did not want to wait until after *That '70s Show* ended before Ashton made the attempt to jump to the big screen. Luke Perry from *Beverly Hills 90210* and James Van Der Beek of *Dawson's Creek* had both failed miserably in their attempt to jump from small-screen to big-screen stardom, in large part because of Hollywood's tendency to stereotype and thus limit opportunities to grow in different areas. The trick, they felt, was to begin the long road to movies now at a gradual pace so that by the time his tenure on television was over he would already be established as a major motion picture star. They saw as their model George Clooney who by the time he left *ER* had already done a number of films and was a known commodity in the movie world.

So Goldberg began hustling Ashton, his marketability, his sex appeal, and his talent all over Hollywood. Studio executives and producers were admittedly cautious in taking him on for even a small part in a major motion picture and rightfully so. He had nothing but a career as a model and a season of *That '70s Show* to show them; and that, on the surface, was a pretty slim offering.

In the meantime, Ashton continued to enjoy the perks of newfound stardom. The teen magazines were the first to notice him, and his face began to grace the covers of *Tiger Beat, Seventeen,* and others with regularity. His circle of friends had expanded to include the actors Melissa Joan Hart and Fred Savage. Ashton was getting to know all the right people and was being seen at all the right places. It was a networking rite of passage for any actor with designs on the future. For Ashton, it was just a nonstop party.

But he had not forgotten where he came from. He was on the phone with his family at least twice a week, regaling them with all the strange and wonderful things that had happened to him in Hollywood. And once he got himself situated, he would go back to Homestead every couple of months for a few days. The trips helped him stay grounded. They brought Homestead more fame and interest than it had ever seen.

Everywhere he went in town, the girls went crazy over him. One local store sold pictures of Ashton. The request by local girls for signed photos was so insistent that Diane had to keep reminding her son to bring more of them on his trips. And with his high profile came the first trickles of media interest. Press coverage was something new to Homestead residents, so people were, more often than not, willing to answer questions about Ashton.

As Ashton's fame grew, so did his business entourage. In addition to Simon and Goldberg, Ashton now had the services of a business manager, a lawyer, publicists both in and out of the studio, and agents who would field commercial and, if he was still interested, modeling assignments. Having his every waking moment controlled by somebody was a new sensation for Ashton, but it was one that he appeared comfortable with.

"I am covered," he related. "What I know is that I don't know anything about this business. And I don't want to have to know."

Professionally, he was growing as well. It had been suggested that Ashton might want to consider acting lessons. It probably would not have hurt, especially since he had designs on being a fully rounded actor who could play many different roles, but he declined, preferring to develop his characters on his own and to learn from his castmates, who ran the gamut from raw rookies like himself to veterans like Kurtwood Smith. Ashton was not afraid to ask questions, and during rehearsals he would work hard to make even the most inconsequential scenes work to perfection.

In April 1999, shortly after the conclusion of the first season of *That '70s Show*, it was announced that Ashton had signed a three-picture movie deal with Miramax. It was a daring move on the studio's part to sign a deal that big with a relative unknown, but everybody involved felt that, in Ashton, they had a diamond in the rough. Miramax was cautious enough to not rush Ashton into a film that he would feel the pressure to carry all by himself.

So they went to the other extreme.

Ashton's first film was a minuscule role in the Ben Affleck thriller *Reindeer Games*, in which he played a character called College Kid in two scenes, in one of which he gets beaten up by Affleck. It was not his film, and he did not have much to do.

All he had to do was look and act like a college kid, so his University of Iowa education had come in handy after all. Ashton looks back on that film as having been a good way to get his feet wet and not much more. Although he did love the idea of being on the set of a big motion picture, thought Affleck was pretty cool, and acknowledged that he would always remember seeing his name on the big screen in the cast list for the first time, in the scheme of things if you blinked during *Reindeer Games*, you probably missed him.

Ashton has often remembered the joy of getting beaten up by Ben Affleck and the opportunity to work, though briefly, at the feet of a great director. "Working with John Frankenheimer was amazing. He taught me more in a week than I learned in two years in college."

The brief appearance in *Reindeer Games* did whet Ashton's appetite for his next film, which was not long in coming.

This one showed more promise. In the Freddie Prinze Jr. comedy *Down to You,* he earned praise for playing a bartender named Jim Morrison who, in his handful of scenes, does a manic turn as a teen obsessed with the dead rock star of the same name. Interestingly, Freddie Prinze Jr. was having a hard time moving to the level that Ashton was already trying for. At this point in his career, he was, like Ashton, trying to move away from lightweight teen material to more mature roles.

Ashton took his first real film role seriously. Sure, Jim Morrison was essentially a one-note stoner with an obsession for his namesake rock star, but Ashton was determined to make the character something special.

In an early indication of his willingness to do whatever it took to get his performance right, Ashton sat down with a bunch of old *Ed Sullivan Show* tapes that had featured the Doors in order to get the late singer's look and mannerisms down. He also developed a solid feel for what was admittedly a minor piece in the *Down to You* puzzle.

"He's not really Jim," he said to an interviewer. "But he always wanted to be Jim Morrison, and his name was Jim Morrison, so he decided that the easy road in life was to be Jim Morrison."

Life on the *Down to You* set was a blast for Ashton. He was hanging out with a lot of young actors his age, and he was learning more about filmmaking. Being on the lower end of an ensemble cast, he did not feel the pressure to carry the film that often crept into his time on the set of *That '70s Show.* Although his character was pretty much laid out in the script, the director Kris Isacsson was big on letting his actors explore their roles. Because of that, Ashton was able to add some subtle shades and depth to what appeared to be a paper-thin cipher.

Ashton's performance was considered one of the saving graces of what was ultimately a lackluster, predictable film, doomed by unconvincing performances and a cliché storyline. The *San Francisco Chronicle* reviewer in particular noted, "The best of the dorm friends is Ashton Kutcher, who looks like Jim Morrison and acts like Jim Morrison."

Again, his work in *Down to You* could be measured only in baby steps. But he showed he was more than capable of handling a fairly substantial supporting role, and his comfort level on a movie set was now as good as it was on the set of *That '70s Show.*

Easily overlooked was his next film performance, the role of Louie in the independent coming-of-age comedy *Coming Soon.* Ashton was part of an eclectic ensemble cast that included Mia Farrow and Jasmine Bleeth. In the role of a young man coming to grips with his and his partner's sexuality, he showed an emerging if flawed comic-dramatic style that engaged rather than annoyed.

Although the elements of coming-of-age sexuality had long been staples in the big studio teen films, *Coming Soon,* with its emphasis on women's needs, had an art-house aura about it that appealed to Ashton. He was asked not to go the stereotypical crazed sex monster route but rather to deal with his own sexuality in more measured terms that emphasized character over broad strokes. It was a film that forced Ashton to work harder.

The film was significant in that it was his first nude scene (tastefully handled) in a lovemaking sequence between himself and the actress Gaby Hoffman. Ashton threw himself into the scene. It was ultimately considered too raw by the motion picture ratings board, which ordered the director Colette Burson to trim the one-minute lovemaking session to ten seconds.

For Ashton, this very small film gave him a taste of the independent world, a universe where cool actors got together not because of the money but for the love of the story. *Coming Soon* was nothing if not an education for the young actor that he long remembered.

In hindsight, it was also an odd choice. After making his entry into Hollywood in such blatantly commercial fare as *That '70s Show, Reindeer Games,* and *Down to You,* moving into the independent art house filmmaking world, where movies are often created on a wing and a prayer and far from the conventional big studio methods, had the potential to confuse. But Ashton proved quite the astute pupil and came off *Coming Soon* a more well-rounded performer.

At that point Ashton was like every other young actor in Hollywood. Having a hit television series and parts in a number of films did not guarantee him instant access to big parts in major motion pictures, a case in point being his audition for the pivitol role of Danny Walker in the big-budget motion picture *Pearl Harbor.* Ashton gave it his best shot but was ultimately rejected for the part that went to Josh Hartnett.

His inability to land it should not have come as a surprise. By acting standards, he was still pretty raw. Good enough for light, largely superficial roles but not yet ready for the challenges of a deeper, more involved character. There was also the dollars-and-cents reality of *Pearl Harbor* that may well have cost him the part. The film had millions of dollars riding on it, so the producers were inclined to go with a recognizable, bankable face whenever possible. His awareness that many in Hollywood still saw him as merely a pretty boy with questionable talent did not seem to faze the actor, who let early rejections roll off his back with little concern.

"I don't think it ever crossed my mind about having this model-actor image," he once told an interviewer. "I think I'm a good actor, so I don't really worry about it."

The result of this early film work was that it was a more polished and mature actor who returned to the set of *That '70s Show* for the second season.

The series remained the perfect ensemble environment in which all the actors were allowed their moment to shine and Ashton to continue to learn his craft in a highly nurturing environment. But it had become clear that the producers knew what they had in Ashton and were taking every opportunity to feature Mike Kelso at least a couple of times in each episode. Through it all, Ashton remained the consummate team player, praising his cast members in every interview and remarking how lucky he was to be around such a talented group of actors who were also such good friends.

Always the supportive partner, Ashton was happy when January's acting career began to take off with a starring role in the TV pilot *Get Real* and a substantial part in the made-for-television movie *All the Rage*. To his way of thinking, her success only served to cement their relationship and also to salve any fears that the difference in their success might jeopardize what they had.

Nevertheless, public statements aside, there was a hint that their both being actors may have had an adverse effect on Ashton and January's relationship. In an innocuous press bio of January for that period, she indicated that she was seeing somebody (Ashton) and that marriage was a possibility if he would allow her to keep on acting. In short, Ashton may have been harboring conservative attitudes toward the relationship and at least below the surface felt that a woman's place was in the home.

Into the second season of *That '70s Show,* Ashton had become, in many people's eyes, the very image of Mike Kelso. Consequently, in press interviews he would inevitably be asked how much he was like his fictional alter ego. Usually good-natured about those questions, he would also be candid in his response: "I am not like Mike Kelso at all. I am not dumb."

Although a lot of people felt he was.

Because of the constant comparison and the intimations in some press articles that he was more lucky than talented, Ashton was eager to come up with a film project that would take him totally away from the Kelso–*That '70s Show* world. He got it during a television hiatus in 1999 with the offer to be part of an all-star ensemble western called *Texas Rangers.*

Texas Rangers, which told the true story of the founding of that real Old West crime-fighting organization, appealed to Ashton on a number of levels. He loved westerns and often bemoaned the fact that so few were being made. The cast, which included Dylan McDermott (on hiatus from his own series *The Practice*), James Van Der Beek (looking for his first non–*Dawson's Creek* success following the lackluster *Varsity Blues*), Rachael Leigh Cook, Robert Patrick, and Tom Skerritt, was the level of actors he was looking to work with. Once again it would be a star-studded ensemble, with little pressure on Ashton to carry the entire load. The movie was to be shot in Canada, which would give Ashton the opportunity to once again travel to exotic locales. Finally it had action, lots of it; at that point that's what the little boy in him craved more than anything else.

As is typical of Hollywood auditions, Ashton was up against just about every young actor that remotely fit the type. Some, he speculated, had more experience and more skills than he did. But when the dust settled the part of the young upstart with a heart of gold was his.

From the first day on *Texas Rangers,* Ashton worked very hard to bring reality to this Wild West role. His character is one of the film's more complex and was part of a love triangle that included Van Der Beek and Cook and all manner of pivotal dialogue sequences. Of course, his being from farm country and having grown up around horses and in the great outdoors gave him a leg up in many scenes opposite more experienced but city-bred actors.

The director, Steve Miner, who had worked around his share of young people at the helm of *Halloween H20* and a pair of *Friday the 13th* movies, was impressed. "He's very concentrated, and he worked very hard. He just didn't stop. He worked real hard at all the riding, shooting, and cowboy stuff."

When he was not doing such difficult and often unpleasant work as spending two days on a scene that required him to roll around in fake rain and frozen cow dung, Ashton took every opportunity to ride off into the Canadian wilderness to see nature firsthand. That like himself, most of the cast were on hiatus from TV shows, also made bonding with his fellow actors easy. After particularly grueling days of gunplay and riding the range, they would often get together and joke about how they could not wait to get back to the relative comfort of a Hollywood soundstage. In particular, Ashton bonded with James Van Der Beek and Rachael Cook. When not riding the range, the trio were almost inseparable, during breaks in the action they were often found huddled in a trailer playing video games.

At the end of what was a grueling filmmaking experience, Ashton returned to Hollywood convinced that *Texas Rangers* would be the film that would turn his career in a different direction.

"I want to keep doing different things," he said. "What was different about *Texas Rangers* was that it was far different from *That '70s Show.* I like being able to showcase my being able to do something other than Kelso."

There was more to Ashton's growth on *Texas Rangers* than getting away from his comic alter ego. The film gave him the opportunity to be an integral part of an ensemble cast, to work with seasoned actors, and to get a feel of what shooting on massive outdoor locations was like. Showing his early dramatic skills in what, for him, would certainly be a big budget showcase reel did not hurt, either.

All of which was by design. For *Texas Rangers,* like every other role he had taken to this point, was a methodical, well-thought-out choice. Meetings of Ashton and his management team were constant and, reportedly, very nuts-and-bolts in their approach to advancing his career. Rather than simply jump at the best money offer with quality be damned, anything Ashton agreed to do, even at this early stage of his career, had to meet certain criteria. The story had to be good, the character he would play had to offer some kind of challenge, and the commercial potential had to be considered. Because the line in the sand had already been drawn. Ashton was not aiming to be just another semirecognizable working actor. For Ashton, nothing short of celebrity would do.

Ashton had long felt that the key to longevity in Hollywood centered on his ability to do a number of things. The possibility of his producing his own films had already come up in many conversations. Obviously, his managers felt he had the smarts to do that job, but they also agreed that his record at the moment did not put him in a position to make demands of that kind.

They also agreed that it would only take one hit movie to change all that.

Given his solid growth experience on *Texas Rangers,* in the can but not yet released, and his reported obsession with reading scripts and taking meetings with an eye toward expanding his career, it came as a surprise that Ashton next chose to do the stoner comedy *Dude, Where's My Car?,* the lowbrow misadventures of a couple of stoned teens who come to after a wild night and can't find their wheels, which contain gifts they had bought for their girlfriends. In their attempts to find their car, they end up in an outrageous adventure full of aliens, wild animals, and no small amount of sophomoric, drug-related humor.

Equally odd was how Ashton got the part. The producer Wayne Rice recalled that during the audition process, he and his fellow *Dude* filmmakers paid a visit to Ashton's home.

"Ashton was doing grouting work in his bathroom while he was receiving guests throughout the evening. He was like this Home Depot guy, a dude through and through."

Audition over. The part was Ashton's.

On the surface, *Dude, Where's My Car?* appeared to be a career step backward. Ashton's role played into the whole Kelso stereotype and was so tied into the teen market that there was no way anybody over the age of eighteen was going to see it. (Or admit to it.)

A lot of people in the industry questioned Ashton's decision to do *Dude, Where's My Car?* However, he made a spirited defense of the film as being a lot deeper than just a bottom-feeding teen comedy.

"It's really silly," he reported, "like a *Dumb and Dumber*–type buddy comedy. It's got sort of Abbott and Costello routines, a little Charlie Chaplinesque comedy; and parts of it are outrageous, like Austin Powers."

The reality was that *Dude* was a logical business decision. Ashton had already established himself as a teen heartthrob with *That '70s Show*. Doing a movie that was not that far removed in character from his established following would keep his name out there and guarantee him his first hit movie in a genre of film that rarely failed at the box office. A hit movie would give him more clout and the opportunity to get a shot at better scripts. So doing *Dude, Where's My Car?* was simply a matter of going with Ashton's perceived strengths.

Which was essentially playing a character not unlike himself.

Filming *Dude, Where's My Car?* was probably one of Ashton's easiest moviemaking experiences to date. The director Danny Leiner was a veteran of television dramas and comedies. He knew how to get the most out of a low budget and a tight schedule. Most important, he was smart enough to let his two stars, Ashton and Seann William Scott, have their creative way with the obviously not very deep material.

The chemistry was good between the two actors, and Ashton in bits and pieces proved adept at improvising his paper-thin cliché of a character. In lesser hands, it would have been easy to dislike the character's stupidity, but Ashton succeeded in twisting and turning the obvious to the point where Jesse became kind of a ragtag antihero that everybody could root for.

"I was heavily influenced by Chris Farley and some of the work he did on *Saturday Night Live*," he recalled. "He had an attitude of not playing it safe and going to the extreme to get the laughs. That was the attitude I adopted for that film."

The film also expanded upon Ashton's ability to do physical comedy. Granted, it was not much more than a lot of running, jumping, and falling down, but it was a definite step forward from the basic shtick he was doing on *That '70s Show,* and it was another aspect of acting that Ashton filed away for future use.

Ashton admittedly had a good time in his first starring vehicle. He got to hang out with real cool people, including the future *Alias* star, Jennifer Garner, in her first motion picture, and, one day on the set, play a real-life hero, when he stopped an out-of-control ostrich from running into a crowd of extras.

However, when all the hype and hyperbole was cleared away, the reality was that Ashton was blatantly playing to his strengths as a light comedic talent. This unfortunately added to the growing impression around town that Ashton, who following the completion of *Dude* went back to work on the second season of *That '70s Show,* was playing with a very limited talent deck.

But like every step in his young career, there was definitely an upside to *Dude, Where's My Car?* For the first time he was the lead in a film. It was a commercially safe bet even if the critics hated it. He would get the lion's share of the credit if it was successful and would dodge the bullet if it bombed. That it would create an image that Ashton would spend years trying to live down seemed unimportant at the time.

None of this seemed to matter to Ashton, because he was still living in a bubble. The attacks on his acting ability had been lightweight and superficial, not the kind of barbs that would rattle an ego or cause a sleepless night. Consequently, Ashton had experienced only the good side. In the back of his mind, he must have sensed that he would eventually take some hard knocks, but with *Dude* in the can, he was living in a state of bliss.

After the rigors of big-time moviemaking, he was happy to be back in the cocoon of his television series and in the familiar, loving relationship with January Jones (a relationship that Ashton had been completely faithful to).

It went without saying that being on a hit TV series and on the cover of every fan magazine on the planet had gone a long way toward cementing Ashton's reputation as one of the sexiest men in Hollywood. But while he could be counted on to be the life of any party and was prone to flirt good-naturedly with other women, Ashton could always be counted on to go home alone or with January.

To that point, Ashton was staying true to his mother's advice on how to treat women: even when rebuffing a woman's advances, he did do so in a way that did not embarrass them or hurt their feelings. This added to the public conception that either Ashton was truly naive and too good to be true or that he was really that dense. Many cynical observers speculated that it would be only a matter of time before he succumbed to Hollywood's temptations and strayed.

The second season of *That '70s Show* showed that Ashton was slowly learning the game of acting. His comedic timing was impeccable, and although Kelso was now being painted in increasingly broader strokes, Ashton found himself instinctively playing the character, adding enticing little nuances when least expected. For good and bad, Ashton often found himself on automatic pilot in playing this dim-witted alter ego. But to his credit, he never turned in less than a highly polished performance.

While the comic rhythms of the show now seemed carved in stone, there always seemed to be an opportunity for Ashton to stretch or have fun. Ashton was big on doing his own stunts, and even such simple things as entering a room and vaulting over a couch became a personal challenge, no matter how many takes were involved. Consequently, while he was never seriously hurt, one could count on the young actor's coming away from an episode with a physical requirement with at least a couple of bumps or bruises.

The chemistry between Ashton and his castmates continued to be strong. After his movie work, he was welcomed back to the show like a conquering hero. He was the first young member of the cast to break out in a big way into movies; rather than harbor resentment, they were totally supportive and happy for his success.

That '70s Show was now a solid, if not spectacular, ratings success and Ashton was the reason for a lot of the attention. The reality was that while truly an ensemble cast, there was an obvious level of excitement in and anticipation from viewers as soon as Kelso entered a scene.

As surveys later indicated, Ashton's appeal ran to both boys and girls. With girls, especially teens, the physical attraction was obvious. With boys, it was the vicarious thrill of rooting for the fumbling guy, much like themselves, who got to hang out, do cool things, and, most important, get the girl. To the viewers of *That '70s Show*, Ashton Kutcher was everyman.

However happy Ashton was with his current comedy status, he was convinced that the world would soon see that there was more to him than Mike Kelso. *Texas Rangers,* due to be released in early 2000, would showcase his skills in a more mature film. He believed it would no doubt do well and open him up to more adult films. But Ashton soon learned another lesson about the vagaries of Hollywood.

According to reports and rumors, Miramax had reservations about *Texas Rangers.* The story was heard in some quarters that the exciting movie the filmmakers had promised was not all that exciting and that it had been sent back to the director for tightening. Also, Warner Brothers, which had its own young western, *American Outlaws,* ready for release, caused Miramax executives to worry that it would cut into their film's box-office potential.

Also holding things up was a legal claim slowly winding its way through the court system by John Milius who had been removed from the film. Whatever the actual reason, *Texas Rangers'* release date was changed four times over the course of 2000 and was finally not released at all that year.

The official line from Miramax was that the studio was just waiting for the appropriate time to release *Texas Rangers* to get the maximum exposure for the film and to capitalize on the collective star power of the movie. Admittedly, action-oriented films did do better during the summer months, but Ashton was not interested in Hollywoodspeak; he just wanted the film on the screen.

An exasperated Ashton said at one point that he was getting tired of announcing the film's release date only to have it changed on him once again. "The opening date keeps changing, and it's turning me into a liar."

However, all his complaining could not keep *Texas Rangers* from sitting on the shelf.

Which meant that the only example of Ashton Kutcher's much-trumpeted new big-screen image to be seen in the year 2000 would be the very juvenile *Dude, Where's My Car?* Ashton was everywhere on the publicity trail for the film, doing the expected softball television and newspaper interviews. Although he had done a lot of press for *That '70s Show,* this was the first time he had to carry most of the weight of the film on his shoulders. The publicity experience was a fun time for Ashton. He was playful and accommodating. No questions seemed off limits. While those interviewing him did not see *Dude, Where's My Car?* as anything more than a B-movie trifle, they came away impressed with Ashton's boyish combination of innocence and candor.

The film opened in the spring of 2000 with a lot of prerelease publicity. As expected, the critics universally despised the film, making only small reference to Ashton's being more than capable of pulling off a big-screen version of Mike Kelso.

The *San Francisco Chronicle* had its tongue firmly planted in its cheek when it reported "*That '70s Show* dolt Ashton Kutcher plays dumb to Seann William Scott's dumber. Together they give himbo-chic a stoner's haze."

The *New York Times* critiqued, "Kutcher and Scott exude an innocuous charm as sidekicks, but compared to Wayne and Garth or Cheech and Chong, or practically any other comedic teams, these two are strictly lightweight."

The *Cleveland Sun* deadpanned, "Ashton Kutcher and Seann William Scott play hopeless stoners spending the movie's entire 82 minutes asking the title question. And it certainly feels that way."

But the critical beating did not stop teen audiences from flocking to the theaters, largely on the strength of Ashton's name on the marquee. Whatever the reason, teens found a lot to like in the sheer dumbness of the story line and the exuberance with which the actors played through it. And while Ashton's and Seann's portrayal of the witless stoners did teeter close to the edge of stupidity, there was also a sense of naïveté that proved attractive. In no time at all, the modestly bud-geted *Dude,* bad reviews and all, was closing in on $50 mil-lion in box-office gold.

Ashton had mixed feelings about the success of his first starring movie. He was glad it was successful, but for the first time, he was defensive at the notion that he was just playing his *That '70s Show* alter ego on the big screen.

"If everything would have gone the way I hoped, *Texas Rangers* would have come out before *Dude,*" he once told a reporter.

Ashton's high TV profile inevitably led to offers to appear as host and or guest on a number of what were considered hip fringe cable-television shows. And if they served in get-ting him to an audience that had not been watching *That '70s Show,* he was there. In the year 2000, Ashton did four episodes of the MTV show *The List,* where he rubbed shoul-ders with musicians and actors from a wide variety of circles. During a hilarious appearance on *WWE Smackdown,* he jawed with wrestlers and learned the ropes of a different kind of acting. Appearances like these were a true high-wire test for Ashton. There was no script, and there was no character to assume. People would either pass on or buy into the whole Ashton Kutcher thing based on what they saw. The consensus was that audiences liked what they saw.

The success of *Dude, Where's My Car?* and the continued high ratings of *That '70s Show* allowed Ashton to flex even more muscle in the movie world. Based on the excellent word of mouth received from the set of *Dude* by the likes of the producer Gil Netter, a deal was struck that would have Ash-ton coproduce and star in a lighthearted comedy romp called *The Guest* (later changed to *My Boss's Daughter*).

The Guest told the story of a young man who tries to get

close to his boss's daughter by house-sitting while his employer is out of town. All manner of broad slapstick humor ensues when a number of bizarre characters decide to drop in. Again, it sounded paper-thin and yet another thinly disguised take on the whole *Dude–'70s Show* universe. But Ashton and his people felt that it was different enough to warrant his interest.

Of particular interest to Ashton was that his character was more of a bumbling straight man than a witless stoner buffoon, which, Ashton figured, would allow him to stretch his acting muscles without venturing too far from the comedic roles that had made him a star.

In his choice of *The Guest*, Ashton showed a conservative streak that was often in contrast to his public statements. He often proclaimed that he wanted to take creative chances, yet he was willing, at least at this point in his career, to take baby steps that would not ask much of him as an actor. Yes, his management team probably had a lot to do with his decisions, and maybe he was simply taking the best of what was offered him. But to many it seemed that Ashton was looking for the quick kill, the big bucks, nothing more.

Because of the nature of the deal, Ashton would not be required to audition for the film, which was to be directed by David Zucker of *Airplane!* fame. The director had been assured that Ashton was more than up to the task and so he was not worried—until the day he was brought in to read with the actresses auditioning to be his costar.

In hindsight, Ashton recalled that the auditions went fine and that he liked the idea of not having to audition himself but rather help pass final judgment, as coproducer, on who would be his costar. But Zucker, as he watched the endless parade of young starlets read with the actor, sensed that something was wrong.

Zucker later related in interviews that the readings did not go well and that a big part of the problem was that Ashton was not very good. In fact, Zucker indicated that he felt Ashton's readings were so bad that he was dreading a shoot in which he would have to spend his time holding this over-hyped actor's hand just to get him through the simplest scene.

However, Zucker did not want to risk total disaster by bailing out of the film or, even worse, telling Ashton he did not think he was much of an actor. So he crossed his fingers and hoped for the best.

During the preproduction phase of *The Guest*, Ashton worked very hard to justify his producer credit. He was very involved in the casting and was instrumental in suggesting that the veteran actors—Ashton favorites—Michael Madsen and Terence Stamp be in the film. And many was the time that an intent Ashton met with Zucker late into the night to give his input in the rewriting of the script. Zucker was pleased with how seriously Ashton was taking the film.

Now if he could only act.

Zucker breathed a sigh of relief once filming started. Ashton, while nowhere near the top-drawer actor that Zucker had been led to believe he was, had magically morphed into at least a competent one who was able to hold his own with both such relative newcomers as Tara Reid and veterans like Madsen and Stamp.

"Once the camera is rolling, he slides right into it," the director stated of Ashton's performance on the set of *The Guest*.

He kept his fingers crossed throughout the entire shoot, hoping against hope that his young star would have enough gas to get to the end of the filming. He was relieved when Ashton not only held on to the slapstick straight man role but by turns would invoke the memory of Peter Sellers and Abbott and Costello in their prime. It was to Zucker's credit that he was able to keep his fears regarding Ashton's questionable talents under wraps during filming, perhaps realizing that any kind of a problem might send the young actor into an emotional tailspin.

Finally, on the last day of the shoot, Zucker approached his young star and laid his cards on the table. He sugarcoated his comments by saying he felt Ashton had done a good job but that he had been worried by the poor audition readings.

Ashton likely did not take the director's comments well.

It was the first time that a filmmaker had questioned his talents to his face. The anger perhaps turned to insecurity, leading Ashton to question his acting talent and if he really had a future in Hollywood. While outwardly he remained his usual gregarious self, inwardly he must have felt the pangs of insecurity. His management team did their best to assure their young charge that everything was fine and that he had done a good job.

It was during this period of extreme self-examination that he confessed in an interview that he might be tiring of the Hollywood rat race.

"I've been thinking of going back to college and getting my degree in biomedical engineering," he said. "I'd really like to do that, and I just might, once I get tired of acting. I kind of like to live my life like Forrest Gump. As soon as I conquer something, I want to go on and do something else."

Although Ashton eventually got over his insecurities, he was determined to be a bit more cautious in what he did from that point on. *That '70s Show* continued to be the safety net that would obviously have a long run and allow him the security to pick and choose just the right scripts. There was the continued frustration that *Texas Rangers* was still not scheduled for release. The success of *Dude, Where's My Car?* had instantly ignited talks of a sequel. And while Ashton would not dismiss the notion out of hand, he was cautious, stating that there were certain elements of the first film that had not been explored to his satisfaction so consequently he had not been totally satisfied with it. He said he would consider a sequel but was not in any rush to do it.

Adding to the reassessment of his life and career were his feelings toward January. To his way of thinking, they would always be good friends, but the feelings of love and devotion he experienced early in their relationship were, after three years, waning.

Other theories were floated for their breakup. One was that Ashton's career having eclipsed January's had put a strain on their relationship. Rumors had spread that Ashton had been unfaithful, but those were proved to be unfounded. Another had it that Ashton, suffering discomfort at the memory of his parents' breakup, was suddenly commitment-shy. Others voiced the opinion that Ashton simply wanted his freedom to date other women and live the life of one of Hollywood's reigning sex symbols.

January was crushed but at the same time realistic about how Hollywood had, in their case, claimed another victim. "Romance is hard in this town," she said.

Not too long after the breakup, Ashton offered the reason why January and he had split up.

"I could have married her. But after three years, I realized she probably wasn't the person I wanted to spend the rest of my life with."

Chapter Five

Wild Thing

Publically Ashton appeared to have weathered the storm of his breakup with January Jones. Inside he was hurting.

It had been the longest romantic relationship of his life. He felt a certain amount of sadness and, because of the way his public statements on the breakup may have been taken by January, a little guilty. He had gotten used to the idea of coming home from a hard day's work and finding someone waiting for him. There were still the reminders of her presence in the things she had done to the apartment, the feminine touches and the aura of a woman's touch that haunted him for some time.

Adding to his personal bumps and bruises was the grow-ing backlog of his motion pictures that had not gotten out to the public. His management team explained to him that a lot of different elements went into the decision of the right time to release a film. Unhappily, Ashton kept cutting to the idea that the reason was that his acting was not up to par. What-ever the reason, all he could do was wait.

Waiting was not an Ashton Kutcher strong suit. By his admission, he was at his emotional best when he was working on something. And despite a daily routine of work that en-compassed nearly twenty-four hours, Ashton was restless and always looking for something to do. His management team sensed this and was always coming up with projects that would interest and challenge him.

Networks usually frowned on their series stars doing guest shots on competing network shows, but Fox, no doubt be-cause of Ashton's growing clout in the business, gave their blessing when he expressed a desire to do a guest shot on his good friend Andy Dick's sitcom, *Just Shoot Me,* in February 2001. In the episode entitled "Mayas and Tigers and Deans, Oh My," Ashton assayed a role not unlike Kelso of a guy who caught the eyes of the ladies on the show. Though the charac-ter was little more than an already-played-out cipher, Ashton gained the experience of working with a regular cast other than his own and fitting his character into the show's differ-ent rhythms and tones. And the response was good. On the surface, it just appeared that Ashton was indulging in yet another take on Mike Kelso, but the reality was that he man-aged to bring some new shading to this stock character.

With each job Ashton seemed to be growing more pol-ished in his execution as an actor. Make no mistake, he was not even close to threatening De Niro or Pacino for the plum roles in Hollywood, but he was showing definite growth. Ashton was happy with his progress, and there was no doubt in his mind that he was now a real actor.

Texas Rangers continued to be a painful subject. The latest report had the film coming out in April 2001. The studio's opinion of the picture had continued to decline, and the entertainment press, smelling a miniature *Heaven's Gate* in the making, was reporting that rather than giving *Texas Rangers* a major promotion followed by a wide release, the studio was essentially dumping it in a mere four hundred theaters with very little promotion. Ashton was to do very little in the way of publicity for the film, a sure sign that to Miramax, *Texas Rangers* would be dead on arrival.

The word on *My Boss's Daughter* was not much better. The studio reportedly was again unhappy with the finished product and would not announce a definite release date. Ashton, perhaps still reeling from Zucker's comments at the end of filming, was once again feeling the sting of professional rejection. Since he had hit Hollywood, Ashton had heard all the stories that questioned his acting ability. He was now concerned that the studios believed them and looked to cut their losses by withholding his films from release or dumping them into theaters with as little fanfare as possible.

Ashton has conceded that in the wake of his breakup with January and his pictures ending up on a shelf, he felt down in the dumps. Once again thoughts of packing in the acting thing and returning to school ran through his head. Fortunately, he had good friends to pull him out of his funk.

Ashton had become tight with the *That '70s Show* cast. He had become particularly close to Danny Masterson and Wilmer Valderrama, with whom he shared the same attitude, newness in the business, and sense of humor. On the set or during off hours, it was not uncommon to see them together playing video games in their trailers, hanging out at each other's apartments, or going out on the town or on weekend trips. And it was that dynamic duo who took it upon themselves to bring Ashton out of his dark mood. With Ashton in tow, they hit the Hollywood party scene with abandon. Ashton found it therapeutic to be out and around other people. The attention of any number of young women also did not hurt his ego.

In a sense, this was Ashton's true coming-out party in Hollywood.

It was the first time since he found success that he was truly free to enjoy all the benefits and perks of being a sexy single television and movie star. Word travels fast in Hollywood, and once it was learned that he was unattached, Ashton had his pick of starlets and hangers-on.

Did he take advantage of the situation? He most certainly did. But any relationships with women at that point were quick, sexually to the point, and usually over very quickly. Ashton often commented during this period that he liked being a Hollywood player. His romantic life in the weeks and months following his breakup were for the most part kept fairly low-profile. Ashton had never been a kiss-and-tell type. But it also seemed a fact that he could not go very long without a steady relationship. He missed the sense of companionship, that somebody he could talk to about something or nothing. Somebody around whom he could be himself.

Enter Ashley Scott.

Ashley, best known now for the short-lived TV series *Birds of Prey*, was a beautiful, exotic-looking model turned actress who at the time was just starting to gain a foothold in Hollywood. Ashton admired her spunk and positive attitude. That she had a good sense of humor about herself and her career were a plus. Ashton was not sure at this point if he wanted a steady relationship. The devil in him was telling him to be a player and that having any number of women in his life was the right thing to do. But then there was this angel.

Ashley and Ashton were instantly taken with each other and quickly became a couple.

Was Ashton, despite playing up his down-home attitude, really a bit of a narcissist who was dating those who reminded him of himself? That he was finding love with only actresses and models might have been the luck of the draw. He was a working actor, so the dating pool tended to be limited to working women in his field.

But that aside, Ashton seemed to instinctively gravitate toward the image of his own personality. Or, if one digs deep enough, the image of his mother. Freud would probably have a field day with Ashton's choices in women. But with Freud not around, it was left to the entertainment press to speculate, and they seemed to approve. Ashton and Ashley were photographed by the paparazzi when they went out on the town, and their names were mildly linked in the gossip columns when they attended a movie premiere or a party.

Behind the scenes, people who monitored the comings and goings of Hollywood's next big thing took notice of Ashton's growing profile. He had not climbed the Hollywood ladder in the traditional, time-honored way. For the most part he had avoided being a pawn in the studio publicity machine. And most important, he did not have to pretend to be somebody else to get his name in the headlines. The people who made their living reporting on Hollywood and the lifestyles of stars on the rise had decided that Ashton Kutcher was somebody who should be getting more attention, so the press set their sights on him.

His relationship with Ashley Scott was the last time his private life was truly private.

The Ashton-Ashley relationship lasted nine months and was a relatively low key affair. Both were working and seemed equally intent on their careers. When they were together, they seemed genuinely happy. Whether it was true love or just the need for companionship, Ashton and Ashley's romantic life appeared to be stress free.

And when it did come to an end, that was also fairly stress free.

Ashton remained mum on his relationship with Ashley. Ashley would acknowledge only that "sometimes you're not quite ready for each other. We were going in different directions."

The consensus in the wake of the breakup was that Ashton was not really ready for a committed relationship with one woman. And although he liked to think that he let all the women in his life down easy, years later he looked back on his relationships and hinted that if he could he would like to go back and fix some of the mistakes he had made.

As always, Ashton's cure for a failed love affair was to bury himself in his work. He continued to read scripts but was careful about agreeing to anything in light of the experience of his previous films. Ashton was anxious, despite his successes always seemingly in a position of having to prove himself. It was a trait that could take somebody a long way in Hollywood, but it was also an attitude that had more than once doomed an actor determined to have it all to a career-ending burnout.

He could have jumped into something if he wanted to.

Scripts were piling up at his front door. Most were garbage, stupid comedy variations on his Mike Kelso character and the guy he played in *Dude, Where's My Car?* Almost all offered obscene amounts of money to sign on the dotted line. Ashton would occasionally be tempted by those less than perfect offerings, preferring to work to sitting idly. But the cooler heads of his management team encouraged him not to rush into anything. Rightly so, none of them were ever made. If he were only in it for the short term, Ashton would probably have said yes to all of them. But because he wanted to be taken seriously as an actor, he said no.

That did not mean that Ashton was not in the public eye.

He continued to build on the audience he had cultivated on *That '70s Show* and *Dude, Where's My Car?* by being the perfect late-night and cable talk-show guest. One of his most calculating moves in that area was to make two appearances on the *Andy Dick Show* in August and September 2001. This cable gabfest and variety show was known for its cutting-edge, often profane approach to television. Nothing was scripted, and guests always had to be on guard for the outrageous line of questioning. For Ashton, it was a chance to hang out with his good buddy Andy Dick. It was also a test of just how sharp he could be as a guest. Ashton proved adept at a more adult brand of repartee and easily fielded the inevitable himbo and sexually charged questions with ease.

Through it all, Jason Goldberg and his management team handled their young client with honesty and candor. They wanted him to work, but, like Ashton, they were looking for projects that would advance his career rather than limit it. They were alternately patient, encouraging, and confident that Ashton was on the brink of something big. And that's what Ashton needed to hear.

Ashton soon pulled out of his creative funk and concentrated on expanding his already strong television base. With Goldberg, he started a production company called Katalyst Productions, which was created primarily to generate television ideas to the networks that Ashton would have varying degrees of participation in.

"I don't have time to be overwhelmed with success," he said at the time. "I'm pretty hyperactive, and what I love to do more than anything is work."

That '70s Show continued to be his refuge, as it continued to have high ratings and was picked up for a third season. There were the inevitable rumors that with the show's success, the cast members would soon be asking for more money. Anticipating that, Twentieth Century Fox quietly and efficiently renewed all the principal actors' contracts with substantial raises. For his part, Ashton had his contract extended through the 2004 season.

The cast of *That '70s Show* continued to work like a well-oiled machine. It did not seem to matter that Ashton had become the breakout actor and was getting most of the attention of the press. On the set they were one big happy family that would, Ashton often said, "basically bullshit on the set all week and then turn out the show on Friday."

Ashton also seemed to finally have a handle on how to play Mike Kelso. He often explained that there was a fine line with the character. People wouldn't sympathize with a character who came across as merely stupid. They would, however, get behind one who was believably naive and gullible, which was the way Ashton chose to play him. So while Mike Kelso continued to come across as a blatantly obvious television type, the effort that Ashton put into the character resulted in a caricature of some substance and depth.

Texas Rangers did finally hit the theaters in April 2001—with a resounding thud. Admittedly, the film was tame, reverting to melodrama at every opportunity and shoehorning in the expected cowboy action almost as an afterthought. Too much time was invested in a love triangle that was patently annoying. Not surprisingly, critics did not take kindly to the film.

The *Austin Chronicle* said, "This movie makes *Young Guns* look like *The Wild Bunch*. Kutcher shows off his ranger togs for his horse, cavorts in threadbare long johns and winds up in a bathtub with James Van Der Beek."

The *New York Post* was equally dismissive. "*Texas Rangers* is no *Unforgiven*. It's more like unforgivable. An utterly anachronistic Ashton Kutcher is the designated comic relief."

The *Chicago Tribune* opined, "An all-sizzle-and-no-steak adventure. Most of the raw-boned young actors look goofy in cowboy gear, and their acting is dreadful."

Audiences, despite the collective star power in the cast, stayed away in droves, perhaps preferring their television favorites in familiar TV surroundings rather than in the unfamiliar confines of the Old West. *Texas Rangers* was in and out of theaters in two weeks. Ashton's ego was bruised by the fate of the film, but by this time he had built up a tough hide.

"I feel like I've become a better actor since I shot that movie," he lamented. "So it kind of bums me out, because I want to give people the best stuff that I'm doing right now."

Personally Ashton was moving on. Among other things this meant moving out of his Hollywood Hills apartment and into a new home on a quiet cul-de-sac in the nearby Los Angeles hills. He acquired the services of a live-in personal assistant named T. J. Jefferson, and he continued to party at the drop of a hat. It was the rare party where he did not have at least a couple of women hanging all over him. It was also the rare party at which Ashton was left completely alone. But, as always, the rumors surrounding Ashton Kutcher's love life were always more interesting than the reality, about which the actor was adament about not saying much. But as the first onslaught of interest in Ashton's love life hit, Ashton himself, perhaps naively, added fuel to the fire.

There was the persistent rumor, started by him, that he was involved with Nicole Kidman in her post-Cruise, pre-Kravitz days. It was a story that Ashton later admitted was closer to fantasy than reality. The story also made the rounds that Ashton has always had his eye on Cameron Diaz. Neither woman ever expressed an interest in Ashton's unsubtle overtures.

Then there was the night midway through 2001 when Ashton and the daughters of the president of the United States got together.

It started the night Ashton and some friends went to a party sponsored by the athletic shoe company, Nike. It was a standard-issue loud Hollywood party. Everybody checked everybody else out. Telephone numbers and business cards were exchanged. Cell phones seemed to flip open and close in unison. However, there was one glaring exception. There were a lot of guys standing around looking like Secret Service agents.

As Ashton made his way through the party, greeting and mingling with old friends and new, he found the reason why. The very much underage Jenna and Barbara Bush were standing in the midst of the crowd, talking excitedly with drinks in their hands. That the two girls were at a hip party where alcohol was served and drugs most likely used was not a surprise. According to numerous press reports the president's daughters were in the middle of their drinking period, and with the everpresent Secret Service agents as chaperones they were living the wild life of the privileged set.

Initially Ashton tried to steer clear of the two Bush girls, especially after one of his friends made a loud, sexually crude remark about the girls within earshot of the Secret Service. He was not in the frame of mind to have government heat in his life.

Eventually, he did meet them, and the conversation got around to what he was doing after the party. When Ashton said he would probably go home, the girls invited themselves along. Word soon spread through the Nike party that the *real* party would continue later at Ashton's house. It was a strange caravan that wound its way through the hills of Los Angeles and back to Ashton's house: Ashton, his new friends, Jenna and Barbara, and, trailing behind, the cars carrying the Secret Service.

Ashton was not used to having his style cramped by grown-ups with guns not well concealed, so he put his foot down, insisting that the agents had to stay outside. He was surprised when they agreed and set up a quasi-perimeter around his house.

The party continued with alcohol and the Bush girls' illegal drinking going on under the noses of the agents. Ashton was feeling paranoid at having the government right outside his door. At one point, he stepped outside to check on his unwelcome guests. One of them walked up to him and asked, in a purely official manner, of course, if the president's daughters would be spending the night. Ashton responded with an emphatic no before stepping back inside. The presence of the federal government in his front yard had suddenly taken all the fun out of the party.

Ashton went looking for the twins and soon found them in a bedroom, smoking from a hookah with one of his friends. Ashton freaked out. This was the kind of situation that could easily get him on the government's shit list. Fortunately, nothing too crazed happened. Jenna and Barbara left at some point in the evening, and Ashton crashed. He never heard from the Bush girls again, though he would jokingly tell interviewers that for a long time after that party he had the distinct feeling that his telephone was bugged.

Word of the party soon hit the gossip columns, with one story reporting that the president was upset to discover that his daughters had been partying with Ashton. Ashton laughed it off but was secretly thankful that the Bush girls' visit did not land him in a lot of trouble.

With yet another hiatus looming on *That '70s Show* in 2002, Ashton was once again restless to give movies another try. The talks centered on a sequel to *Dude, Where's My Car?* were nowhere near the serious stage. And although the idea of breaking away from comedy to do a straight dramatic role appealed to him, he dismissed the rumor circulating around Hollywood that he would be offered the starring role in the next Superman movie by saying, "I don't want to do sequels." (Unless, he said, it was a sequel to his own work.)

Most observers of the entertainment industry thought he was crazy for turning down even a chance of playing the Man of Steel. They continued to think that some months later when he likewise looked down his nose at the rumor he was about to be offered the role of Batman. There was more than a hint of superstition in his not considering the roles. He felt that there was a curse connected to the actors who had done Superman, and that most of the people who had played Batman had gone on to relative degrees of obscurity.

This turned out to be Ashton's spin on things. It was later reported that he was nowhere near the top of the list to play Superman and that, once he was ready to come on board, Batman's director, Christopher Nolan, rejected him as a Batman candidate.

Finally he settled on yet another youth-oriented light comedy, called *Just Married*. The movie, which would costar another up-and-coming actress, Brittany Murphy, centered on the comic misadventures of a newly married couple, a high-society girl and a blue-collar average Joe whose marriage and love are tested through all manner of misadventures in the United States and overseas. *Just Married* was a broad, slapstick farce, another commercially safe teen romp. But Ashton saw enough potential in the material to stretch beyond the Kelso character, so he agreed.

And Ashton had more than *Just Married* on his mind.

His production company had been working overtime to come up with a television program for him to produce. They finally came up with the ideal series for the MTV generation, a *Candid Camera* meets *The Jerky Boys* ambush-style show called *Harassment*. At that point, *Harassment* was conceived as a gross-out adult version of *Candid Camera*, with no celebrity connection other than Ashton's producing and writing and appearing on camera as the ringmaster of the pranks. It was with that attitude that the pilot episode showed the reactions of a husband and wife in a hotel room who discover a mutilated corpse in the bathroom. Unfortunately, the couple not only did not get the joke but threatened to sue MTV on the grounds of emotional distress. The concept was quickly retooled and renamed *Punk'd*.

The *Punk'd* concept was old school, TV with more than a hint of hip modern nihilism. Ashton and a group of guerrilla cameramen would prank Ashton's many celebrity friends in ways designed to bring out the most distress.

The idea was simple, and, when the show premiered on MTV, it became an instant hit, as Ashton pranked his celebrity friends and acquaintances in a variety of outlandish situations that inevitably had them cursing, crying, or making obscene gestures for the enjoyment of millions of viewers.

Among the most notorious of the *Punk'd* episodes was the one in which Justin Timberlake is convinced that his possessions, including his pets, were being confiscated by the IRS for back taxes. Frankie Muniz having his sports car stolen in front of a fancy restaurant and Pink being told that her boyfriend had just been arrested for running an automobile chop shop were also first-season highlights.

On the surface, *Punk'd* seemed the latest chapter in television's perceived descent into hell that had been started by the likes of the *Jerry Springer Show.* What Ashton logically concluded was that the audience had gotten tired of celebrities' being thought of as infallible and above them. Bringing them down a notch and making them go through things that happen to real people on an everyday basis was a stroke of genius. What *Punk'd* would do to his relationship with his celebrity friends remained to be seen.

The immediate success of *Punk'd* put Ashton in the hot seat. Word quickly got around that their good friend was liable to prank them for his show, so it would become more and more difficult to get the pranks to work. There were also not well veiled threats of getting even with him by pranking him. But the show continued to flow, the laughs kept on coming, and Ashton seemed to find no end of opportunities to put one over on his celebrity friends.

Punk'd was an instant ratings success, and, even before the first season ended, Ashton had already agreed in principle to do a second season for a substantial increase in pay. The negotiations were low key and quick. In the end, Ashton and MTV both got what they wanted.

When not acting in *That '70s Show* and producing and starring as chief prankster in *Punk'd*, Ashton was very much the party guy. He was often seen at A-list parties and was a regular at courtside at local NBA games. He was getting just enough sleep (reportedly in the neighborhood of five hours a night) to do his work, and despite being a consummate meat eater and chain smoker, he was healthy.

With *Punk'd* an almost instant ratings winner, even by MTV and cable standards, Ashton was now looking again to the big screen to push the envelope. It seemed that he had been saying thanks but no thanks to the many *Dude* and *That '70s Show* knockoffs forever. But still the offers for lightweight and downright insultingly stupid fare kept coming his way. In a sense, Ashton had only himself to blame.

"I do comedy out of choice," he once said. "It's fun to do, and they make people laugh."

Ashton finally happened upon a project that seemed to be his way out of stereotyping, a fantasy thriller called *The Butterfly Effect*.

A cross between *Back to the Future* and *Jacob's Ladder, The Butterfly Effect* tells the story of a troubled young man who tempts fate by going back to when he was a child in an attempt to change his life and the lives of others. Unfortunately, what he discovers is that everytime he goes back in time, he changes his own present and that of those around him. Despite the surreal concept of the film and the story's numerous unsettling moments, Ashton liked the idea that it was very much an actor's piece rather than a special-effects extravaganza and that the title character was flawed and human in a way far removed from anything he had done. He was also intrigued by the downbeat ending in which his character commits suicide (an ending that was softened by the time the film was completed).

"I didn't know if people were going to accept me as a dramatic actor," he stated. "I felt like I could do it, and I felt like I could do it well."

But he also knew that attacking a project so extreme had inherent risks. Ashton was known for comedy and nothing else. His one stab at a legitimate drama, *Texas Rangers,* was his least-talked-about film. Fans loved him as the dumb guy with a heart of gold. Would they give him a chance in something that was light-years away from comedy or would they stay away in droves? It was a chance that Ashton, in an ongoing battle against the anchor of Mike Kelso, felt was worth taking.

"The more risk you take, the more reward there can be," he once told an interviewer.

Given his rising star power, he was also able to negotiate a coproducer's credit for the film.

"It's not like I wanted to do a movie that's not a comedy," he said in defense of his decision to do the film. "I want to surprise people. People don't think that I can handle a dramatic movie. So I want to be good. I want to be great."

Amy Smart, the costar of *The Butterfly Effect,* later acknowledged the intensity with which Ashton pursued the role. "He wanted to be seen in a different way. He wanted to be challenged and to have something drive him."

There was a lot in the history of Hollywood for Ashton to stake his claim at a shot at this dramatic part. Actors like Tom Hanks, Robin Williams, Bill Murray, and Steve Martin had started out as comics and were able to make the jump to dramatic roles. But Ashton was not going to rely on precedent to land him the part.

Ashton lived and breathed *The Butterfly Effect* for weeks, rereading and dissecting the script until the haunting images of the characters and the story line were embedded in his brain. If the opportunity to read for the film came his way, Ashton would be prepared.

The filmmakers, however, were not so easily convinced. The lead character in the film was an average guy who was serious and the consummate loner, roles Ashton had not come within shouting distance of.

"While we were casting *Butterfly,* we looked at everyone in Ashton's age range," said the film's codirector, Eric Bress. Bress and his codirector, J. Mackye Gruber, had good reason to be careful whom they chose for the pivotal role of Evan. The pair had been making the rounds of movie studios with their script for *The Butterfly Effect* for seven years before finding a studio willing to take on the edgy subject matter and also allow them to direct. Bress and Gruber were thrilled when New Line Cinema did. They were not thrilled when, after countless auditions had stalled development, New Line very strongly suggested Ashton Kutcher for the role.

"I had seen *That '70s Show,* and my first reaction was, 'I don't think he's smart enough for the role,' " recalled Bress. Gruber was even less impressed, buying into the myth of Ashton Kutcher as male bimbo.

Gruber added, "When the suggestion to use Ashton Kutcher was thrown at us, we were like, 'No way he's in the movie.' That was really a bad suggestion. We thought, 'No way *Dude, Where's My Car?* is going to be in our movie that we've been fighting for all these years.' We were basically forced to go have this meeting with him."

Bress and Gruber grudgingly arranged for a meeting with Ashton. Since this was going to be a meeting, not an actual audition, it was agreed to keep it low key. So the directors obliged Ashton by driving to his home. Their feeling going in was that they would go to his house, talk a while, and find that he was truly not what they were looking for. Everybody would go away happy.

The directors later disclosed that Ashton was not as advertised, that it was the classic case of judging a book by its cover. The directors found him to be surprisingly focused, that he could definitely play a serious part, and that he brought a real enthusiasm to the project.

"Everything he had to say, all the questions about the script were so insightful," related Bress. "He had really dissected the script and had a firm grip of the story and character."

Ashton liked where Bress and Gruber were coming from. He had only one basic question for them. "My biggest question was were they trying to make a freaky thriller or were they trying to make something smarter than that?"

The writer-directors convinced Ashton that smarter was the way they wanted to go with *The Butterfly Effect*. They shook hands, promised to be in touch soon, and left Ashton's house.

"We walked out of the house," recalled Bress, "got in the car and said, 'I think we got the guy.' "

Ashton was grateful for the opportunity as well as for the opportunity to finally break the Kelso curse. "I would say that I'm a character actor and that all the comedy I've done has been comedy characters. I'm thankful for the directors not judging me on what I haven't done yet."

Instinctively, he knew that the pressure was on him, and

he prepared for *The Butterfly Effect* as he had never prepared for a film role before.

"I spent about two months just researching the role," he said. "I was checking out psychology books. I got a wheelchair at my house for the scenes that I'm in a wheelchair and practiced moving around. One day I even disguised myself and rolled through a mall just to see how people look at somebody in a wheelchair. I was doing different things to prepare myself for the different levels of the character."

His preparation did not stop there. He arrived at the Vancouver, Canada, location of *The Butterfly Effect* a week early to get himself mentally prepared for the role. "For that week, I wasn't talking to anyone, including my family. I remember calling my dad a couple of weeks before I went up to Canada and warned him that I wouldn't be calling him for a couple of weeks. I felt like I had to be this guy the first day I walked onto the set."

While waiting for filming to begin, Ashton continued his research. For scenes in which his character would have to deal with the seedier elements of society, Ashton and his costar Amy Smart disguised themselves as street people and went down to a Vancouver neighborhood notorious for its drug activity. For hours they stood there, observing junkies, drug dealers, and others of a criminal persuasion as they went about their business to get a feel for certain character types.

Amy later recalled the uncomfortable nature of their research. "It was definitely a dangerous situation. There were heroin users and crack addicts all over the place. It was disturbing."

The chemistry between Amy Smart and Ashton was integral to the success of the film. The two actors seemed like a good professional fit. Like Ashton, Amy had been playing essentially a certain type since coming to Hollywood, and she was looking to *The Butterfly Effect* as her ticket to meatier roles. They had hung out in the same Hollywood circles and had reportedly dated briefly. Amy was convinced she could pull off the role but later admitted that she was curious about how Ashton was going to handle the downbeat material. She and the rest of *The Butterfly Effect* crew were about to find out.

Ashton was not taking his producer title lightly. He had input into the casting of the film and script changes, many were necessitated by his entry into the film. As conceived by Bress and Gruber, *The Butterfly Effect* was geared to a more adult audience, with much adult dialogue and scientific and supernatural jargon. The directors wisely acknowledged that with Ashton in the film and his fan base being a lot younger and unsophisticated some of the dialogue would have to be simplified.

The Butterfly Effect went before the cameras in May 2002. There was a certain amount of tension on the set. Even after a strong audition, Ashton came to this film with a lot of baggage. His comic roots showed but not much else. From the directors on down, the unspoken words on the set were "show me."

And he did.

Ashton reached down deep inside for this role. He had done comedy almost nonstop since he hit town, and even the dramatic range he showed in the ill-fated *Texas Rangers* was slight compared to the range of dark emotions he would have to display in *The Butterfly Effect*. Those privy to his work on the film reported an amazing transformation. Gone was the one-note comedic actor. In his place was somebody who, while not perfect, showed some considerable dramatic chops as a tortured soul who uses his own brand of time travel to try to set things right.

Among those suitably impressed and more than a little surprised was his costar, Amy Smart. "I had only seen Ashton do comedy. This was the first dramatic thing I had seen him do. From the minute I stepped on the set I saw how much work Ashton had put into it."

One of the biggest challenges Ashton faced on *The Butterfly Effect* was that two other actors would be playing him at a younger age. Since all of his scenes as an adult would be shot before the child actors did their scenes, there was the challenge of making the grown-up character look and move like his younger counterparts. Ashton would sit, talk, and even walk with the younger actors so that every mannerism they had could be duplicated by him. Makeup and a beard added to the tortured look, and Ashton took great pains to put himself in the proper frame of mind. This was not the role to come across as less than believable or subconsciously winking at the camera. Evan Treborn was a tortured soul. Ashton had to feel that way as well.

It was his willingness to go the extra mile that instantly endeared him to the directors and the rest of the cast and crew. Most of the crew had a preconceived idea about Ashton, and it was not all good. They were expecting the good-looking former model and the guy who played all the dumb characters. What they got was an actor willing to do whatever it took to make the best film possible.

Predictably, *The Butterfly Effect* was not a tension-free ride for Ashton. He was dealing with two firsttime directors while trying to maintain a firm grip on a character that was always teetering on the edge of madness. Ashton sensed that they would eventually lock horns. Sure enough, voices were raised.

Everybody wanted his or her way. Compromises had to be reached.

"I was really freaked out," he reported. "But they were accepting, and they let me try anything I wanted to try. They also told me when I sucked."

And although he was amiable enough with the cast and crew before filming began, Ashton was very much into the role once the cameras began to roll.

"This character I played was pretty disturbed, and what was tough was that in order for me to be confident when the cameras were rolling, a lot of the time, in between scenes, I had to stay focused on what we were doing, and I couldn't be screwing around."

When it came time to shoot his scenes, the actor became a different person. In the past it had been a small leap to attach any film role Ashton played with his Kelso counterpart on *That '70s Show*. But with *The Butterfly Effect*, Ashton seemingly transformed himself into a character totally removed from that big, dumb alter ego.

And he was excited at the ease in which he could suddenly leave the confines of obvious comedy roles behind and immerse himself in the darkest of dramatic characters. Whether *The Butterfly Effect* was successful or failed at the box office, Ashton knew that he was already a winner.

Ashton was the closest he has ever been to a monk during the filming of *The Butterfly Effect*. He was normally so emotionally drained by the end of the shooting day that all he wanted to do was go back to his room and go to sleep. It was a rare time when he went out on the town for a little excitement. And even in Vancouver, the paparazzi were around to chronicle his every movement.

Ashton later claimed that he had been so into his role that

he was lucky if he went out once a month during the filming. Yet all the pictures floating around gave the impression that he had been out partying every night. Ashton took every opportunity to try to set the record straight, but ultimately people were going to believe what they wanted to, and Ashton soon realized that he was fighting a losing battle.

He could not wait for this film to be seen. Unfortunately, in the vagaries of Hollywood filmmaking, *The Butterfly Effect* was, like *Texas Rangers* and *My Boss's Daughter,* put on the shelf and on hold for the indefinite future. The consensus was that the film would most likely be released in early 2004.

Ashton continued to freelance on the small screen. In May 2002, shortly before doing *The Butterfly Effect,* he appeared in the episode of the sitcom *Grounded for Life* entitled "Dust in the Wind," essentially playing his bemused, befuddled self. That he was good on other shows and in other situations was not surprising. As he matured as an actor, Ashton had developed an uncanny ability to mold his personality to any character.

Consequently, Ashton was very much in demand on all fronts. That added substance to the consensus that he was not long for *That '70s Show.*

But Ashton continued to state that he loved it and would stay as long as it was a comfortable fit for him and the show's producers. "Why," was anybody's guess. He had long since outgrown the need to do it, and his career would not suffer if he left at this point.

But it appeared that Ashton was pragmatic enough not to jettison a sure thing before another one came along. That his movie career had been inconsistent may have had something to do with his decision to stay. Maybe it was the age-old actor's fear that he would never work again. It could have been that his old-school attitude made him feel loyal to the people who had given him his big chance. Whatever the reason, Ashton stayed put.

"I'll definitely do *That '70s Show* for at least another year, and then we'll see," he stated. "The guys on this show are like my family."

Ashton, following the completion of *The Butterfly Effect,* returned to *That '70s Show* seemingly reenergized. After the complexity and the challenges of the film, he welcomed the simplicity and predictability of the sitcom, and it showed. The cliché of Mike Kelso was still evident, but Ashton's growing prowess as an actor allowed him to do more, in subtle ways113, with the character.

Despite the notoriety of *Punk'd,* Ashton continued to thrive in the middle of a gaggle of celebrity friends. Justin Timberlake, despite his *Punk'd* experience, remained extremely close, and he got along famously with Jack Osbourne, son of the metal maniac, Ozzy. Easily one of his most pivotal alliances took place midway through 2002, when he made the acquaintance of the infamous rapper, Sean "P. Diddy" Combs.

P. Diddy had entered the entertainment spotlight with a lawless reputation. He was a known player who had dated Jennifer Lopez and had had several run-ins with the law. He was arrogant and had a big ego.

Consequently, Ashton and P. Diddy seemed like the oddest of odd couples: the street-smart rapper and the naive Iowa farm boy. It seemed more like a *Saturday Night Live* skit than an actual friendship. Amazingly, the pair hit it off immediately. They were often seen courtside at basketball games or cracking each other up at parties. They would often get together at the best restaurants in town. In the often delicate celebrity arena of perception, style, and mutual respect, Ashton and P. Diddy had connected.

"There's nothing I can't tell him," Ashton once said, "and there's nothing he can't tell me."

It was alleged that P. Diddy had taken some heat from his more hardcore rapper associates for aligning himself with this white-bread sitcom star. But P. Diddy shined them on. Nobody was going to tell *him* whom he could hang with.

Hooking up with P. Diddy was also a sign to many that Ashton was moving up to a glitzier circle. It was evident that his rapper buddy was influencing him, the main thing being that Ashton, long known for his informal style of dress, was now dressing in a hipper, more formal, more street style. Much was made in the press of Ashton's newfound fashion sense with side-by-side photos of him before and after. It would have been laughable if it weren't that just about everything Ashton wore fit him perfectly and that he looked so good in them.

In deed, the pair got on so well that they announced that they were going to form a modern-day version of the Rat Pack, in homage to the fifties and sixties group of carousing entertainers that included Frank Sinatra, Dean Martin, and Sammy Davis Jr. It seemed like the idle boast of a pair of young men who had it all and were free to do what they wanted. (To date the new Rat Pack has turned out to be all talk and no action.)

Just Married began filming in the summer of 2002. Ashton found the filmmaking experience one of his best: working with a director with whom he was in synch on how to play this often perplexed newlywed and enjoying the many outdoor locations in Europe. That he got along so well with his costar, Brittany Murphy, and that on camera the chemistry was so good between them was a happy bonus. During their time off in Europe, the pair were inseparable, clowning around in the countryside or on the hilly slopes. They were like two kids in a candy store. And the best thing about it was that it was all strictly business and totally platonic.

Ashton was aware of Brittany's recent personal and professional history. After appearing opposite Eminem in the acclaimed movie *8 Mile,* Brittany had a short personal relationship with the outrageous rapper.

It was a relationship that was fairly well documented in the press, one that if you believe the newspaper accounts did not end well for Brittany. The story was that the relationship with Eminem had completely shaken her trust in men and relationships and that she had made it plain that she was not interested in another movie-set romance. This was fine with Ashton, who was definitely not interested in an onscreen romance developing into something off screen, so he went into *Just Married* with the idea of keeping things on a professional, "just friends" level.

Professionally, these were chaotic times for Ashton. He was in the middle of the current season of *That '70s Show* while attempting to do *Just Married.* When he kissed Brittany on camera, all he could think of was what the next line of dialogue was for Mike Kelso. He was so distracted, and with so little time to hang out, platonic was the best he could offer, even if he were thinking otherwise.

Platonic seemed to work. From the first day of rehearsals it seemed that it would end up being that way. They would talk when they had a chance and immediately felt comfortable with each other. Both felt the chemistry would work for the film.

"I knew we had something," recalled Brittany. "I knew that it would make an impact on my life."

True to their hopes, *Just Married* turned out to be a fun-filled, creatively fulfilling time. The jokes and one-liners were working. The physical slapstick timing of the film was perfect. Ashton and Brittany were believable as the perplexed newlyweds. If there was any sexual tension between the pair, it was there only for the camera.

"We were friends first," Brittany recalled of the *Just Married* shoot. "I didn't look at him that way, and he didn't look at me that way."

Despite their best efforts, however, friendship turned into something else.

"When we were doing the movie, we were just friends," Ashton insisted. "Then we just kind of started out hanging out more."

The consensus on the set was that, no matter how hard they tried to hide it, Brittany and Ashton were already a couple before filming ended. They were often spotted holding hands and cuddling. It was hard to tell where the film couple left off and the real couple began (which may be the reason why the more intimate scenes between the two actors are probably the best things about the film).

By the end of the movie, the good-friends relationship had evolved into a classic movie-style romance.

"The movie ended up being a success because of our off-screen chemistry," declared Brittany. "It wasn't something I ever could have planned."

Later the actress declared that "Ashton had reaffirmed my faith in relationships. I'm really in love and it's the greatest feeling."

Whether planned or not, Ashton and Brittany were very much an item by the time *Just Married* wrapped. Surprisingly, they were able to be together away for the most part from the prying eyes of the paparazzi for some weeks before announcing their relationship in October 2002.

To the press at large Ashton and Brittany seemed like the odd couple. At five feet one, Brittany was dwarfed by the six feet three Ashton. But what those interested in celebrity romance discovered was that the couple, emotionally and otherwise, was a perfect fit.

Despite their years in the business, Ashton and Brittany were still naive about the interest and intrusions of the press. For them, press interest and photographers were a validation that their careers were on the rise, so they felt that any intrusions on their privacy was a small price to pay. Their dealings with the media pertained to previous relationships (Brittany had received the lion's share of the attention as a result of her liason with Eminem) had been mild. They saw no real need to hide.

So when they came out as a couple, they really did. Everywhere they went they seemingly courted the prying eyes rather than attempting to avoid them. It was not uncommon in the early days of their relationship to openly kiss, hug, hold hands, and make out when they knew a camera was documenting their every move. That their privacy was being invaded did not seem to enter into either of their heads. They were both still very childlike about their romance, in a sense winking at the camera while showcasing their love. Sure, it was serious, but it was also fun and games, and, professionally speaking, it surely did not hurt the publicizing of the upcoming *Just Married.* The two stars of a movie falling in love during the making of the film? It was a press agent's dream.

The line between a real relationship and a public exercise in lust was being blurred. And while at the drop of a hat they professed love for each other, neither seemed sure whether it

Ashton at the Hollywood Film Festival's Gala Ceremony and
Hollywood Movie Awards—October 7, 2002.

PHOTO BY JANET GOUGH

Ashton Kutcher
and Ashley Scott.

PHOTO BY

MIRANDA SHEN

Brittany Murphy
and Ashton Kutcher.

PHOTO BY

GILBERT FLORES

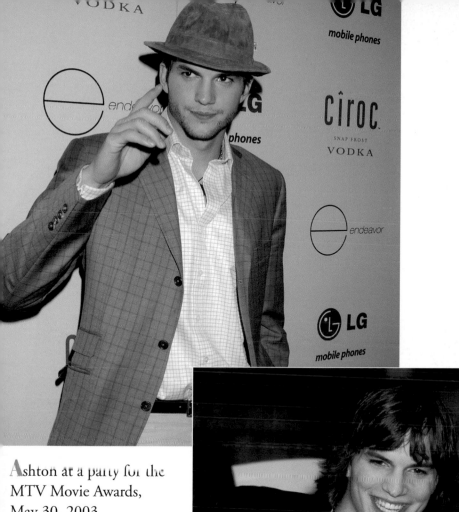

Ashton at a party for the
MTV Movie Awards,
May 30, 2003.

PHOTO BY

GILBERT FLORES

Ashton at the 1st Annual
TV Guide Awards,
February 1, 1999.

PHOTO BY MIRANDA SHEN

Ashton at *GQ*'s March Issue
Party, February 16, 2000.

PHOTO BY MIRANDA SHEN

Ashton and sister Tausha.

PHOTO BY JANET GOUGH

Ashton at the Maserati Pre Golden Globe Kick-off Party,
January 16, 2003.

PHOTO BY MIRANDA SHEN

Ashton with Demi
Moore and her
daughters Tallulah
Belle and Scout.

PHOTO BY

GILBERT FLORES

Ashton with Bruce
Willis, Demi Moore,
and their kids at the
*Charlie's Angels: Full
Throttle* premiere.

PHOTO BY

GILBERT FLORES

Ashton Kutcher
and Ashley Scott,
July 9, 2001.

PHOTO BY

GILBERT FLORES

Ashton Kutcher
and January Jones.

PHOTO BY

ROGER KARNBAD

Sean "P. Diddy" Combs and Ashton Kutcher.

Demi Moore and Ashton Kutcher.

was love or pure physical attraction that had brought them together. Which was why, when the inevitable marriage questions came up, they really did not have an answer.

Once while in New York, the couple agreed to let a *New York Times*' writer and photographer tag along on a night on the town. While the photographer snapped away and the reporter furiously jotted notes, Brittany and Ashton cavorted shamelessly, saying outlandishly complimentary things about each other and holding tight on to each other. That it would receive extensive coverage in the *New York Times*' upscale style pages appeared to be nothing more than an inside joke the two of them shared.

With them making no attempt to hide it, their relationship had become a hot item along the gossip and tabloid trail. Pictures of the couple being openly affectionate were everywhere, as were breathless reports of the couple's latest liason. Speculation ran high as to whether this was love, lust, or just a great big publicity stunt. While stopping short of calling their relationship anything, Ashton did relate that "I like everything about her. She's the total package."

It was comments like that one that perpetuated the theory that Ashton liked the idea of being in a relationship but was still not ready to commit to one woman.

Late in 2002 Ashton finally gave an indication that there might be more to their romance than smoke and mirrors when he took Brittany home to visit his mom in Homestead. For the trip, he chartered a private plane, one used by such stars as Eminem, Paul McCartney, and U2's Bono, to fly them to Iowa. It was a stealth operation that caught the paparazzi completely off guard.

Brittany was excited at the idea of meeting Ashton's family, but on the two-hour flight, she was also very nervous. For openers, she was not crazy about flying. And she was not sure what the trip meant in terms of their relationship. Ashton was perhaps not sure himself. But that he wanted his mother to meet Brittany seemed to indicate that, unlike with Ashley Scott and the other women who had passed through his life, this was more serious.

Ashton's mother later reported that she was suitably impressed with Ashton's new love, with the emphasis on love. "Are those two even acting?" she said in an interview after the visit. "They act the same way here at home. They're always holding hands, goofing around, wrestling around on the floor like people in love do. It makes a mother proud to see someone actually care for your child as much as you do."

Whether they were acting or not, the couple were finally beginning to tire of the media attention and the paparazzi who now stalked them consistently wherever they went. After an attempt at a quick getaway in Australia in which they were mercilessly followed by photographers, Brittany sarcastically stated, "We forgot our cameras, but we still ended up with all our vacation pictures."

The Ashton-Brittany romance was not played out completely in the public eye. Occasionally, they were able to sneak off to do the kinds of things that normal young people do away from the prying eye of the camera lens. A big thing was to sneak off to a drive-in in Pasadena, where they would park in the back, munch popcorn, and do what young people do at a drive-in. In a more public outing, they had a favorite bowling alley in Los Angeles where late at night they could often be found.

On the surface, their relationship had all the earmarks of the rare Hollywood love match that might just work out. Professionally, they were at the same stage in their careers.

They understood the pressures of being in the public eye and for the most part were comfortable with their lives and each other.

So comfortable that Ashton agreed to accompany Brittany back to her parents' home for a holiday get-together. Brittany's parents were impressed by Ashton and gave their blessing to the relationship. In the spirit of the holiday season, Ashton made a New Year's resolution to give up smoking. Perhaps he believed it was not going to stick, because he said, "At least I'll try, and everybody knows that God loves a tryer."

The strain of being the hot Hollywood couple began to show in January 2003, when Ashton and Brittany were faced with publicizing *Just Married* in endless press interviews. They wanted to talk up the movie, feeling that it contained some of their best work and hoping against hope that *Just Married* would reach a larger audience than the predicted teen market. Unfortunately, the press were only interested in hearing about their real-life romance and the persistent rumors that they would soon be married.

While he avoided the personal questions at all costs, Ashton's true feelings about Brittany would occasionally seep through, such as during a softball interview with a local teen magazine.

"I'm not dating anyone, but I'm definitely in love with someone," he said. "And I don't even know if she knows how much I'm in love with her."

Ashton's admission was surprising. Normally, he was not one to make his personal feelings public. That he expressed his love for Brittany so freely made a strong case for their love being real.

The night of the *Just Married* premiere was vintage Hollywood, with the walk down the red carpet and the choreographed stops to pose for pictures and chat with the more influential members of the press. Ashton managed that night to avoid most of the media's personal questions as he made a beeline for the safety of the theater. But Brittany was asked if the story line of *Just Married* had any connection to her current real-life relationship.

"It's definitely a real-life romance at this point," she said. "But beyond that I can't say. I'm not a psychic, I'm an actor."

Emotionally, Ashton and Brittany seemed to be on the same page. They were in love. What they would ultimately do about it was another matter. Publicly, there had not been any talk of marriage. Privately, it was anybody's guess.

Just Married opened in February 2003 to the typical Ashton kind of reviews, decidedly mixed ones that seemed to take great pleasure in trashing the film but were not quite as brutal when it came to Ashton's acting.

The *Chicago Sun-Times* said, "*Just Married* is an ungainly and witless comedy."

Empire magazine was typical of the mixed reviews when it stated, "The flimsy material is elevated by the comic talents and likeability of the leads."

The *Syracuse New Times* said, "Kutcher is a lanky pratfaller who is capable of bringing clueless innocence to an art form level à la Gracie Allen."

Film Threat said the film was a mixed bag, "A head on collision between some nice performances and a really stupid plot. Kutcher has a real zeal for comedy and a certain down to earth charm that's appealing."

In point of fact, *Just Married* was, hands down, Ashton's best comic turn to date, easily eclipsing *Dude, Where's My Car?* The on-screen chemistry between the now off-screen lovers was real. The comic turns were plentiful and carried a sense of timing that can come only from sea-soned actors.

The film was number one in box-office earnings its open-ing weekend and went on to gross $56 million by the end of its initial theatrical run. But by then, Ashton and Brittany's relationship was crumbling. The couple was seen together less often in public; when they were, they were reportedly less af-fectionate. At a March 15 charity event in Los Angeles, Ash-ton was asked if Brittany and he were going to get married.

His response was a resounding no.

However, well into March, Ashton continued to put a positive spin on their relationship and always talked up Brit-tany and himself in a way that made one think that they were still very much an item.

"Things are totally great with us," he told a reporter in March. "When we go out, we hang out with our friends and stuff."

If it seemed that Ashton was waffling on the status of his relationship with Brittany, perhaps he was. Part of him liked the idea of love and romance and being with one partner, and part of him no doubt still chafed at the prospect of being tied down when he could be enjoying the attention of a lot of women. There were also rumors of a growing personality conflict between them. Ashton was still very much the party animal who wanted to be out all night every night, while Brittany had reportedly reverted to being a homebody. There were also stories circulating that Brittany's mother, Sharon, had taken too much of an interest in her daughter's romance and to Ashton's way of thinking had become a busybody.

Ashton was perhaps also thinking that the romance, born in the emotion of making a movie, had finally run its course. He was having trouble making a decision about Brittany and where their relationship was heading. Finally, he did.

The couple called it quits in April 2003.

Ashton did not appear to take his breakup with Brittany Murphy as hard as he did that with January Jones. This led to speculation that for him it had only been a fling and nothing more, but he felt strong enough about Brittany's feelings that he refused to rehash the relationship and the breakup in the press. He did concede in a recent interview that he had learned one important lesson from his relationship with Brittany. "I wouldn't recommend dating coworkers. It's not smart. At all."

However, Ashton was not through commenting on love and relationships. Around the time of his relationship and ultimate breakup with Brittany Murphy, Ashton espoused a very liberal line to a British reporter. "I enjoy casual relationships because I don't like to feel pinned down. Calling yourself a couple can lead to trouble, arguments, and jealousy. If I'm going out with someone, the rule is we can be with anyone else if we feel the need—as long as we're honest. Whirlwind romances always fizzle out."

There was a sense of resignation in those comments. It was as if he were trying hard to make it ring true. But given his background, to many it sounded like the kind of things Goldie Hawn used to say to justify her lack of success in relationships early in her career. Ashton was not one to take lightly failure of any kind, and perhaps that quote was a way to appear above it all. What he was actually feeling at that time remains a mystery.

What is known is that Ashton was not shy about announcing his breakup to the world. In fact, he did it on national television when Regis Philbin, the morning talk-show host, asked him about his love life, and Ashton announced that he was definitely now single.

Shortly after the breakup with Brittany Murphy, Ashton was once again the subject of romantic speculation, this time with Britney Spears. But like most of his romantic encounters, it was simply a matter of the pair being at the same party and talking for a minute, nothing more, although one tantalizing tabloid item indicated that the pair spent some serious time together and that Ashton had been spotted coming out of Britney's house on at least one occasion. Ashton and Britney pretty much laughed those reports off as pure fiction.

During this period it was also reported that Ashton was dating the actress Monet Mazur and the Los Angeles nightclub owner Jen Goldman. Little is known of either relationship. With Goldman, it was reported that they dated only a couple of times, that was all. The Mazur relationship consisted largely of a road trip to Las Vegas where they were spotted dancing at an Oasis concert and holding hands at an out-of-the-way table at a club called the Baby's Lounge. But these encounters did not last long and were not serious. The public's continued fascination with Ashton's love life seemed to have taken on a life of its own, which, Ashton reasoned, was going to make having any kind of future relationship out of the public eye difficult at best.

Ashton was stuck. Publicity is the life blood of any star's career. But he was beginning to see how difficult having every aspect of his life be public property could be. Reading and hearing things that were not true and having to deny them had become a chore. Reading and hearing things that *were* true but also were, to his way of thinking, none of anybody's business had become an ordeal.

But while he could not avoid the press completely, he could try to isolate himself from it. Once a free spirit when it came to interviews, Ashton was now more choosy about whom he talked to and cautious about what he said. An avid reader of the tabloids and fan magazines, he stopped looking at them all together. He also cut back on his consumption of the entertainment television shows.

In the days following his breakup with Brittany, Ashton was once again free and easy. For a lark, Ashton, his *'70s Show* buddies Danny Masterson and Wilmer Valderrama, the actor Colin Hanks, and others in his fun-loving crew flew down to New Orleans for a couple of days of fun and games at Mardi Gras. For Ashton this was a good time. The bar-hopping, carousing, and just experiencing the wild times at the wildest time of the year was a tonic that made him feel alive. Ashton and his posse did not get much sleep, so it was an exhausted group that dragged themselves back on the plane for the flight back to Los Angeles.

The plane taxied down the runway and took off. By the time it had reached cruising altitude, everybody was either asleep or very close to it. Then trouble.

At 32,000 feet, the plane suddenly lost air pressure. The cabin was without sufficient oxygen for twenty minutes. Ashton, Danny, and Wilmer, after securing their oxygen masks, woke the others who had lapsed into various stages of unconsciousness and helped them get their masks on. The plane made an emergency landing, then proceeded on to Los Angeles. Nobody was injured, and Ashton was declared a hero for his quick thinking in the emergency that possibly kept his buddies alive.

"It's scary. It's freaky," he said after the incident. "But I got right back on a plane to go to Europe. You can't really be afraid of living."

Throughout the month of April, Ashton continued to cook on all burners. When he wasn't working nonstop on

That '70s Show and *Punk'd,* his production company was working overtime on other TV ideas that would involve Ashton on a production level.

With his good friends Danny Masterson and Wilmer Valderrama, he took the entrepreneurial plunge when they became investors of a trendy new West Hollywood restaurant called Dolce Enoteca Ristorante. For Ashton, investing in the restaurant was more of a lark than anything else. He liked to eat, and he liked the idea of being part-owner in a place he could hang out in. These seemed like good-enough reasons. That Dolce Enoteca would ultimately turn out to be wildly successful and one of the hottest celebrity watering holes in Los Angeles was icing on the cake.

What these and other activities finally proved to Hollywood was that Ashton Kutcher was not really a big, dumb model who had gotten lucky. They were finding that there was a keen business sense behind that innocent look, one that was always on the prowl for ways to expand his personal and professional fortune. A large part of the credit for his budding business acumen rested with his management team. In his own mind, Ashton thought they could not teach him how to act, but they could most certainly educate him on how to invest wisely and how to maximize his career moves. In Ashton they discovered that they had an apt pupil and a quick study.

And one who could be crafty and ego-driven in negotiations. Ashton did not play hardball in business dealings. He played by a less confrontational set of rules. If he did certain things, it was simply for the amount of money that made him comfortable. He either got what he wanted, or he did not play ball. It was a tactic that worked more often than not, with the result that the barely twenty-five-year-old actor being now considered a baby mogul whose net worth was speculated to be in the millions and that the cars, house, and all the material perks of stardom were actually believed to have come through hard work.

Ashton had heard the stories. He did not want to become a statistic; he was determined not to become one of those tragic true Hollywood stories about actors who blew millions and wound up with nothing. But he was also not above spending his money on a good time for him and his friends. One had to be quick to beat Ashton at picking up the check at a high-class restaurant. Once, after a night out with P. Diddy and his friends, Ashton woke up and calmly settled a restaurant bill to the tune of four thousand dollars. On one of his frequent visits to Homestead, he purchased a brand-new car for his mother.

Just when it seemed that things could not get any better, Ashton hopped on a plane to fly to New York to host *Saturday Night Live,* hang with P. Diddy, and live the high life.

Chapter Six

Down with Demi

A shton always enjoyed his times in New York. His professional roots were there, and a lot of friends from his modeling and, now, acting days were still around. New York and Los Angeles were light-years apart to Ashton's way of thinking. There was a sense of cool winding its way through the streets of the Big Apple—its clubs, its restaurants, and its hip hangouts—that was far from the glitz and often paper-thin glamour of Los Angeles. He loved the idea that the weather could change at a moment's notice. Ashton thought of New York as a place where he could lose himself in the crowd and really be himself.

Or, in his *Saturday Night Live* appearance, a place where he could make fun of himself.

Hosting *Saturday Night Live* was a big deal. To land that gig, you needed a couple of things going for you. You needed a degree of fame or notoriety, and you needed an ego and sense of humor up to the task of spoofing yourself and your image. With Ashton, that meant doing his opening monologue dressed only in white briefs.

Ashton loved the idea of poking fun at himself in this extreme manner, so during the days of rehearsals leading up to the show on May 3, he threw himself into the spirit of the show and by all reports was charming in dealing with the regular cast and crew and diligent in crafting his dialogue for extreme laughs. At night, he was out on the town meeting and partying with old friends and new ones.

The press was aware of Ashton's *Saturday Night Live* appearance, so much like in Los Angeles, the paparazzi were there to chronicle his every move. But rather than be annoyed, Ashton chose to just ignore them, so his time in the Big Apple was relatively stress free.

It was during his trip to New York that Ashton made the acquaintance of Demi Moore.

Ashton has often explained that even though he primarily dated actresses, he was clueless, at least initially, about the fame of a woman he was involved with. And so while it is a safe bet that he was aware of Demi Moore, he was not drawn to her by her fame.

How the pair actually met is open to speculation. Some believe it was in Los Angeles just after the breakup with Brittany Murphy and that he had struck up her acquaintance while in the company of his cohorts from *That '70s Show*. Others claim it was at a New York party thrown by P. Diddy the week he was rehearsing his *SNL* appearance. Still others say that the two met informally backstage at *Saturday Night*

Live. However it happened, one thing was certain, Ashton was immediately smitten with the much older actress.

"She was the hottest actress in Hollywood when I was growing up," he once gushed of Demi Moore. "I was in love with her when I was ten."

That was no idle statement. When he was a child in Cedar Rapids and later in Homestead, Ashton made a point of catching all of Demi's films, either on television or video. It was an interesting parallel. Ashton was well into puberty at the same time Demi moved up the ladder from such films as *St. Elmo's Fire, Ghost, Nothing but Trouble,* and *About Last Night . . .* toward the more sexually aggressive roles in *Striptease, Disclosure, Indecent Proposal,* and *G.I. Jane* that marked the zenith of her career and no doubt occupied many of the teenage Ashton's dreams.

But he later said that the first time he met Demi, he was totally in the dark. "I've seen all her movies. But the first time I ever saw her, I didn't know what her name was or who she was. I sat and talked to her for a half hour, not having the slightest idea I was sitting with a famous human being. I don't go around looking to meet famous people."

Nor does Demi. In contrast to Ashton's lifelong fixation, it is doubtful that Demi had ever happened upon an episode of *That '70s Show* or had gone into a theater playing *Dude, Where's My Car?* or *Texas Rangers.*

So it was a safe bet that when Demi laid eyes on Ashton for the first time, the reaction was more lust than love. And who could blame her? But looking to rob the cradle was nothing new for Demi.

Since her divorce from her action-hero hubby Bruce Willis, Demi's choice of paramours has run toward such younger men as the actors Owen Wilson, Toby Maguire, and

Colin Farrell and the studio executive Guy Oseary. After con-
cluding a lengthy relationship with the much younger martial
artist Oliver Whitcomb, Demi, who had then recently
emerged from an acting hiatus to do a small role in the film
Charlie's Angels: Full Throttle, was apparently looking to spice
up her love life with yet another boy toy.

People magazine's Michael Fleeman was one of the many
entertainment journalists who were all over the Demi-Ashton
relationship from the beginning, and while it did get tongues
wagging, to him it was not that big a deal.

"She's a beautiful, glamorous woman, and he's a good
looking guy on the way up," he said in a television interview.
"So why not?"

The reason the Demi-Ashton hookup did not set tongues
wagging was that May-December romances are not uncommon in Hollywood. Witness the ongoing relationships between Harrison Ford and Calista Flockhart, Michael Douglas
and Catherine Zeta-Jones, and Woody Allen and Soon-Yi
Previn. And while not as common, there have also been a
number of older women-younger men romances in Tinseltown, among them the famous, if short-lived, relationship between Cher and the pizzamaker Rob Camilletti, Mary Tyler
Moore and Dr. Robert Levine, and Ralph Fiennes and
Francesca Annis.

So while the Ashton-Demi situation was not unheard of, a
lot of people were quick to paint it in an unflattering light.

Cynics immediately pointed out that the road to Hollywood was littered with celebrity relationships and marriages
that seemed ultimately to serve no other purpose than to
gather publicity and give one or both partners a higher professional profile. Ashton-Demi seemed to fit that profile. She
was an actress who had been away from the business for sev-

eral years and was hungry to get back in the public eye. Ashton was a young actor looking to be seen as an A-list celebrity rather than somebody known for dumb teen movies.

The one everyone cited as an example of what could happen when word of Ashton and Demi hit the streets was the circus that Ben Affleck and Jennifer Lopez had become, one that had gone beyond simple media interest to something larger than life and ludicrous. Other suspected liaisons came to mind: Michael Jackson and Lisa Marie Presley, Anne Heche and Steve Martin, Anne Heche and Ellen DeGeneres. In some circles, even Ashton and Brittany's relationship remained suspect.

All early observers of their budding romance could do was watch and wait.

Initially, "fun" appeared to be the watchword in the relationship between Ashton and Demi. Neither, it appeared, was looking for more than a good time. Both were fresh from relationships and were likely cautious at the prospect of falling in love. For Demi, there were the feelings of her three children to consider. But from the moment they met, electricity arced between them.

As a purely physical attraction, what was there not to like? To say that Demi had kept herself in shape into her forties was an understatement. She had made a point over the years of showing off her body. And whether through the reported "work" she had recently done or through her dedication to physical fitness, Demi could still give most twenty-year-olds a run for their money. Ashton was in his physical and sexual prime. It went without saying that the inclination for the pair would be to get up close and personal.

The first public glimpse of the budding May-December romance came when Ashton was in New York doing *Saturday*

Night Live. The pair was spotted at the oh-so-trendy Dorsia nightclub, dancing together in a sexually charged manner and apparently not caring who was watching and what they were seeing.

"I don't think they knew anyone was really watching them," recalled Michael Lewittes, *Us* magazine's news director, of the early days of their romance.

Early in May, Ashton did his *Saturday Night Live* appearance. He proved adept at even well-scripted and rehearsed stand-up, was relaxed in cavorting onstage in his underwear, and showcased a solid delivery. Demi was reportedly backstage that night, eating up his performance.

By this time the first inkling of the Ashton-Demi romance had hit the gossip columns. The tone of the gossip items was typically salacious. But rather than keep their relationship hidden, the couple seemed to go out of its way to court the press. And the press soon discovered that it was going to need frequent-flyer miles to keep up with the bicoastal lovers.

The couple eventually made their way to Los Angeles, where in mid-May they were discovered dining behind closed doors at Dolce Enoteca, the restaurant Ashton had invested in. Security around the couple was tight, but those who caught glimpses of the pair entering and leaving the restaurant reported that Demi was dressed in skintight blue jeans and that the couple were looking very happy.

"People started getting suspicious that there was something going on at that point," suggested Lewittes.

The Ashton Kutcher–Demi Moore relationship was now on full public display, and media watchers were lining up on both sides of the issue to weigh in with opinions. That yet another Hollywood romance, despite the age-difference angle, was of interest to the public was nothing new. Celebrity romances and breakups were the lifeblood of the tabloid press and gossip columns. It is an element of Hollywood that never goes away, which meant the media would be all over it. And speculating on what it meant.

In looking back on the beginning of their relationship, Ashton admitted that despite the press's interest in his previous relationships, he was blind to what getting together with Demi would mean to the outside world. "I was kind of warned that this would happen," he said in a talk-show interview. "A friend of mine said people were going to flip out over this. I said, 'No, they're not.' "

There were the cynics who continued to insist the whole thing was one big publicity stunt that had been arranged in a calculating bid to move Ashton up from B-list to A-list celebrity status and to give the always publicity friendly Demi a surge for her upcoming appearance in *Charlie's Angels: Full Throttle*. (Representatives for Ashton and Demi denied that there was an ulterior motive.)

It was at this juncture that Ashton got the first relationship questions in interviews. Being asked about his love life was nothing new, but that an older woman–younger man relationship would be such a big deal to the press was a totally foreign notion to him. Being an honest person, he candidly told people that, yes, they were seeing each other and that was it. Unfortunately, what Ashton discovered was that his love life was a big deal and a story that would not soon go away.

And, as always, the public lined up to vicariously live the romance along with the press. Tabloids with early pictures of the couple together flew off the newsstands. The *ET*'s and *Extra*s of the television world led with the latest exploits of the couple, and ratings were up.

Ashton and Demi had become the prime target for the paparazzi cameras, with good reason. The interest in the couple was so high that photos of them together were reportedly being gobbled up by the tabloids and gossip magazines for fifty thousand to one-hundred thousand dollars apiece.

The circus had come to town, and Ashton and Demi were in the center ring.

Ashton later analyzed the public interest by saying that they were curious about something that appeared different to them. "What people don't understand is that we can derive a lot of joy spending time together and that the age thing doesn't matter to either one of us."

After his devastating comments on the set of *My Boss's Daughter,* it was surprising that director David Zucker, of all people, weighed in with support for the couple. "Demi Moore may have fifteen years on him, but Ashton is very mature and focused for his age," he said.

A point well taken. For while his public image was still that of a not very bright, immature actor, the reality was that in attitude and business sense Ashton Kutcher was wise beyond his years and most likely the intellectual equal of Demi Moore. And despite the image she projected in recent films as a flamboyant exhibitionist, behind the scenes Demi had proven to be an astute businesswoman, one smart enough to stake her claim on the production side of the successful Austin Powers films. The joke at the time was what could they possibly have to talk about once they got out of bed. The answer? Probably plenty.

As the relationship progressed Ashton occasionally discussed Demi with the press. His remarks were mostly couched in gushing praise and respect. "She's an intelligent, sexy woman."

But these comments early in the relationship were few. Perhaps Ashton felt that this was going to be a serious relationship, and while he could not avoid some of it being public property, he was not going to run the risk of damaging it through overexposure. The reality was that the Demi-Ashton relationship, fewer than two months old, was already verging on overexposure and becoming the butt of jokes by radio and television talk-show hosts. The public was a whole different matter. People eagerly awaited the next tidbit and photo. As far as Ashton was concerned, the publicity genie was already out of the bottle.

Following their dalliance in Los Angeles, the two lovers hopped a plane for Miami, where they spent some time alone at the Mandarin Oriental Hotel. By this time, the paparazzi were out in full force, dogging their every move. Throughout their stay, Ashton and Demi took to sneaking in and out of the back door of the hotel in an attempt to avoid the prying eyes.

While in Miami, the couple hooked up again with P. Diddy, who seemed to take no small delight in their romance and was willing to do anything he could to help them be alone. On May 22, Ashton and Demi dined with P. Diddy at an upscale, very private restaurant. The next day the rapper offered them the use of his private yacht to cruise leisurely to the Bahamas and enjoy some privacy. Those idyllic days on the yacht and the islands was chronicled by an army of photographers who seemed to always be just one step behind the lovebirds, always within camera range.

Although the world pretty much knew what was going on, Ashton and Demi chose May 31, the night of the MTV Movie Awards, to take their romance public. Typical of Hollywood, their coming out was way over the top.

In dramatic fashion, Demi was on her way down the red carpet when Ashton suddenly appeared, took her by the hand, and led her into the show, as a shocked press corps blasted away at them with cameras as they slowly made their way inside. The scene seemed totally planned and choreographed, but it had the desired effect. Within twenty-four hours images of Ashton and Demi together, holding hands, appeared in publications throughout the world.

The big coming-out campaign did not stop there.

Those backstage at the awards show watched as Ashton and Demi made out with each other as if there were no tomorrow. Once they came up for air, they continued to openly flirt with each other during the awards show. After it, Ashton and Demi joined others at a party hosted by P. Diddy. Throughout the evening, partygoers were treated to the spectacle of Ashton and Demi all over each other. At one point they were spotted emerging, in a highly disheveled state, from a darkened hallway with sheepish smiles on their faces.

Rumors were flying at this point, many of them centered on Demi's former husband, Bruce Willis. Willis, who had previously been silent on Demi's postmarriage relationships, was now reportedly upset at her dating the much-younger Ashton. This only served to fuel the fires of the paparazzi, who were now hoping to get a shot of Willis and Ashton in a fight.

But the hottest couple in Hollywood was well ahead of the curve in that line of thinking.

One can only speculate that once their relationship became serious, Demi felt obligated to introduce Ashton to her ex. In a role reversal of when the guy takes the girl to meet his mother, Demi must have felt it important that Bruce, with whom she still maintained a good relationship, meet and approve of the guy who was going to be with her and with their children.

In early June, Demi and Ashton traveled to her residence in Hailey, Idaho, where Ashton reportedly met Bruce Willis for the first time. After an initially formal feeling-out process, much like two bulls before butting heads over the love of a cow, the pair bonded and instantly became good buddies. With Bruce's approval, Ashton and Demi were about to create news all over the world.

There was much fanfare surrounding the June premiere of *Charlie's Angels: Full Throttle* in Los Angeles. Even though she was not the star of the film, the appearance of Demi Moore and, most likely, Ashton Kutcher on the red carpet was a big reason for the press to turn out in droves.

But you could have knocked them over with a feather when Ashton, Demi, her three children, Rumer, Scout, and Tallulah Bell, and Demi's ex, Bruce Willis, came strolling down the carpet in a friendly group. Questions peppered the group as cameras flashed. Bruce, in an unexpectedly highly evolved state, said that he thought Ashton was a good guy and that he had no problem with his being with his ex-wife and around his children.

Once again Ashton and Demi had hijacked a public event and made it their own. This self-serving performance reportedly ruffled the egos of the film's costars Drew Barrymore, Cameron Diaz, and Lucy Liu. It was their film and should have been their night to shine. They were allegedly angry with the way the photographers had swarmed over Ashton and Demi and had given them the lion's share of the press.

Ashton and Demi continued to take their very public love match cross-country through the summer months. When things got too hot for the couple in Los Angeles in the wake of the *Charlie's Angels* premiere, they took off early in June for a quiet weekend at a remote cabin in Hailey, Idaho, not too far from Demi's home. Ashton and Demi reportedly made no attempt to keep their heat for each other private, and those happening by the cabin reported seeing the pair making out like teenagers.

While in Hailey the couple created yet another stir when they attended the annual awards ceremony of her children's school. All eyes were on them as Ashton and Demi entered the gymnasium where the ceremony was being held. As one parent in attendance put it, "You could almost feel the vibration going through the gym when they walked in."

For a quick trip back east in June, primarily to help publicize the East Coast opening of *Charlie's Angels: Full Throttle,* the couple was everywhere. On one particularly busy night, they started out at a reception for fashion designers who included Stella McCartney and ended up the evening partying at the Cafe Luxembourg with her *Charlie's Angels* costars Cameron Diaz and Lucy Liu, who had apparently forgiven the couple for the one-upmanship at the Los Angeles premiere.

In August, in another display of bizarre family unity, Ashton, Demi, the children and, once again, Bruce, went to Las Vegas to celebrate Scout's twelfth birthday. It was a zany couple of days as the family tried to have a semblance of a good time while sneaking in and out of back doors to avoid the assembled paparazzi.

Brittany Murphy had been devastated by the breakup with Ashton, but she had moved on with her life, was in another relationship, and had continued not to speak publicly of her relationship with him.

Until the night she appeared on *Late Night with David Letterman.*

Although she was there to promote another project, Letterman, long known as somebody willing to dig dirt at the drop of a hat, immediately launched into questions about her former relationship with Ashton and what she felt about her ex's romp with Demi Moore. It was obvious from the look on her face that Brittany did not want to rehash an old relationship for the public's consumption; for her, the memory was still uncomfortable. But Letterman persisted. Brittany thought about an appropriate response for a few moments. Finally she said, "I suppose the crux of their relationship means to him that age doesn't matter and to her that size doesn't matter. Good going for him, I suppose."

There was an audible gasp then laughter in the audience after Brittany went public with Ashton's alleged lack of manhood. She instantly realized what she had done and tried to save the situation by saying she had only been teasing. "They're great, and he's great," she stammered. "Just not for me."

Too late, word of Brittany's remark spread like wildfire and quickly got back to Ashton, who said that Brittany had obviously been joking around at his expense, which was fine with him. As for Demi . . . she had no complaints.

Not long after their relationship began, the press spotted Ashton and Demi dancing up a storm at the upscale White Lotus Club in Los Angeles. This night was typical of the routine that had become the public part of their romance. They dashed into the club amid a wash of camera flashes. Inside, they tried to relax and be themselves while knowing full well that all eyes in the place were on them. Then it was another mad dash out the door for a quick getaway amid more camera flashes.

By this time speculation was running even higher that their whirlwind romance was nothing more than a publicity stunt designed to further both their careers. The couple were not so naive as to think that going out in public was not going to bring the paparazzi around like sharks in bloody water. That they continued to court the press coverage only seemed to fuel the rumors that the relationship was not to be taken seriously.

On the surface, Ashton continued to take the constant media assault with good humor. But the reality was that the constant intrusion by the press into his every waking hour, fueled perhaps by the part they played in his previous relationship with Brittany Murphy, was making him angry. And in an interview conducted during this period, the frustration with being a media target spilled over.

In a number of interviews he compared the paparazzi to stalkers and once thought about resorting to a childhood toy, a potato gun, to keep them away.

"Sometimes I want to punch these guys in the face," he said of the constant paparazzi attention. "They're belligerent. I get paid when I go on the talk shows. I feel the magazines should start paying me to take my picture."

Part and parcel of being involved with Demi Moore was that Ashton also spent a lot of time around her three children, which had the potential of creating conflict with their father and Demi's ex-husband. But the civility on Bruce Willis's part continued, even when it became obvious that Ashton was taking over many of his fatherly duties.

With Demi and her children now spending so much of their time in Los Angeles, Ashton was often spotted taking the kids to and from school, to soccer practice, and even attending parent-teacher conferences. If they had a question that needed an adult answer and their mother or father were not around, they would often go to Ashton. "Being a part of molding someone's life is an incredible thing," he said of playing surrogate parent to Demi's children. "It's an unbelievable addition to my life."

A big part of the media overkill that continued to haunt the couple during the summer months centered on the belief that neither Ashton or Demi was laying their cards on the table. Was it love or lust? After only a few months, the chances are it was more the latter than the former. But with neither side willing to go public with his or her true feelings, the press, and more important, the rumor mill, was free to go hog wild.

Stories about the couple were falling like rain. Some were true. Demi had indeed bought a $3.5 million mansion within jogging distance of Ashton's home so that she could be closer to her boy toy. The couple had allegedly been spotted looking for rings. Ashton had reportedly asked Demi to marry him. According to rumors, the couple was considering having a baby. Each rumor was more outrageous than the previous. It was all very laughable. It was overkill.

Which is not to say that this was all Ashton and Demi's fault. Yes, they were seemingly going out of their way to court the attention, but a lot of the blame must be laid on the lazy level of celebrity journalism, even by gossip-tabloid standards, of those covering the scene. Rather than probe for interesting stories about Ashton and Demi, the reporters seemed totally fixated on their relationship to the point of constantly asking the same one or two questions over and over. Of course, the tabloid press would doubtless respond by saying that this is what the public is interested in. So in the case of Ashton and Demi, there was clearly a lot of blame to go around.

Behind the scenes, their respective camps were not thrilled. In point of fact, the whole Ashton-Demi story had quickly gone from megainterest to megaboredom. From a public relations point of view, there was a real danger of Ashton and Demi following in the tracks of Jennifer and Ben and becoming the couple everybody loves to hate or, even worse, laugh at.

Which was why Demi's handlers delicately told the actress that the media was getting oversaturated with her public displays with Ashton and that she should, if not cool the relationship, at least keep it out of the public's eye. It is doubtful that Ashton's people acted the same way. For whether by design or accident, Ashton's love life had elevated his public profile to unimaginable heights. Even people who had never watched *That '70s Show* or seen any of his movies now knew everything about him, perhaps more than they cared to.

While his peers in the industry tended to look upon the Ashton-Demi media blitz with either amusement or knowing recognition of what can happen, nobody took any direct shots at Ashton for the publicity purge, at least not directly.

Ashton's good friend Topher Grace, while not naming names, recently looked back on the Ashton situation with an unsympathetic eye. "A lot of actors are their own worst enemies. I have certainly seen that in peers of mine. You can get yourself taken out of contention for roles if they know too much about you."

Amy Smart said, "It was great to work with Ashton before all the personal hype happened. A relationship like that doesn't appeal to me."

Whether good or bad, the relationship's publicity had a good effect. A previous deal with the producers of *That '70s Show* had locked Ashton up through the 2003 and 2004 seasons. Now, with his public persona so high and the very real possibility that Ashton was considering leaving the show for the big screen after his contract was up, the producers quickly offered him a big-money extension to 2005 that would effectively bind him to *That '70s Show* for the expected seven-season run. Ashton signed on the dotted line for a reported five million dollars that broke down to approximately two-hundred fifty thousand dollars per episode, reportedly more than twice what any other *That '70s Show* cast member was making. But if they had any complaints about Ashton's raise, they were not saying.

Ashton's castmate, Topher Grace, later revealed that both Ashton and he had planned to leave the show after their contracts ran out in 2004. But they had decided to stay on one more year because they had felt they had only begun to be good actors halfway through the run of the show and wanted to do one more season to "leave the people wanting more."

My Boss's Daughter continued to be a sore spot with Ashton. Owing to lingering doubts about the quality of the movie and Ashton's acting in particular, it had been on and off the release schedule a number of times. The studio continued to float such stock reasons as the right month to open and the perfect opportunity to capitalize on Ashton's popularity.

Suddenly, the film was a definite go for August. Those who had seen the completed film figured it was being dumped to capitalize on the Ashton-Demi publicity. Ashton was glad it was finally getting into theaters, but he proclaimed to anyone who would listen that seeing the film would not be an enjoyable experience.

"I don't want to look at it. I don't want other people to see it. I feel like I'm a much better actor now."

With Ashton's negative comments leading the way, it was

not surprising that upon its release *My Boss's Daughter* received scathing reviews and soon disappeared without a trace. But while the film took a beating, the reviews in many instances at least gave Ashton's acting skills the benefit of the doubt.

The *San Francisco Chronicle* was evenhanded in declaring "Someday Ashton Kutcher will appear in a movie that justifies his hot status. Kutcher keeps this lousy comedy from complete disaster."

The *Village Voice* said, "Those foolhardy or Kutcher-crazed enough to brave the multiplex will discover nothing more than a movie that wants to make you laugh."

The *Pittsburgh Tribune-Review* weighed in with "Too many unfunny scenes of the boy of the moment, Ashton Kutcher."

And finally the *New York Post* blasted the film by saying, "Even Kutcher's staunchest fans will find little justification for enduring this movie."

While an admitted dud, Ashton did come across as a likeable everyman who had made the most of some pretty lame plot points and unfunny situations. It was not his finest hour, but those looking at the wreckage of that film could see that Ashton was making strides as an actor.

Ashton put aside the attacks and continued to work, dividing his time between *That '70s Show* and the preparation for the second season of *Punk'd,* which had lined up a stellar group of victims that included Hilary Duff, Usher, Katie Holmes, and Tommy Lee.

Likewise, Ashton's lackluster movie record did not keep other offers from pouring in. By midsummer he was overseeing some fine-tuning on *The Butterfly Effect,* which centered on adding a more upbeat ending to the film, and was being courted by star directors for A-level motion pictures.

Cameron Crowe was considering Ashton for the lead in his drama *Elizabethtown* opposite Kirsten Dunst, and Steven Soderbergh was considering him for parts in a couple of upcoming projects. M. Night Shyamalan also tabbed the actor to be part of the ensemble cast, to include Sigourney Weaver, Joaquin Phoenix, Adrien Brody, and William Hurt, of his supernatural tale *The Village,* in which a small community in 1897 Pennsylvania discovers that a race of mythical creatures is living in the nearby woods.

That Ashton had taken on coproducer chores on *My Boss's Daughter* and *The Butterfly Effect* and was making production credit a condition on many of the films being offered was another sign of his doing everything possible to escape the stereotype of the bubbleheaded Kelso from *That '70s Show.* While he admitted that the films' executive producers had done most of the real work, his sitting in on casting sessions and learning the realities of film budgets and schedules had been an eye-opening experience.

"I wanted to follow through on the producing process and see the results," he said. "Just doing it is the best sort of training I could get. I've learned some of the hard decisions that have to be made and what it means to come in on time and on budget."

Ashton's plate was full to overflowing, and while he had no intention of slowing down his manic pace, he was overheard saying in interviews around that period that he would have to eat more vegetables, get more sleep, and cut down on cigarettes as a concession to his speeded-up life and lifestyle.

Ashton's faithfulness to anyone he was seriously dating had never been called into question, even though he was notorious for having a roving eye and did not discourage the advances of women in his single days. But all that changed in

September when Ashton was discovered at the Miami restaurant Prive having a quiet evening with the rich party girl Paris Hilton. Ashton's publicity people were quick to spin the discovery as nothing romantic. Ashton said that he was just out having some fun. Demi never acknowledged the incident, and it quickly passed from the front pages. But it did bring into question just how innocent everybody's favorite country boy actually was.

The film remake of *Cheaper by the Dozen* came Ashton's way at about this time. It was a safe production, the kind of film that studios typically release at Christmas to cash in on the feel-good sentiment of the season. Ashton wanted to do it because it would have given him the opportunity to appear in a film with Steve Martin, a favorite of his since the early days of *Saturday Night Live*. And as it turned out, it would have given him an opportunity to hang out with his old buddy Tom Welling, who had a part in the film. But his schedule was so tight that it did not seem possible. Eventually, a compromise was reached that allowed him to do a cameo as a dim-witted, self-absorbed boyfriend. At Ashton's insistence, it was an uncredited role, but fans soon found out.

Ashton's short time on the set was of concern to the rest of the actors: they thought that he would use the film set for a *Punk'd* gag, so a degree of good-natured paranoia and uneasiness permeated the set throughout his stay.

There was also a moment of high drama when, on his first day on the set, Demi showed up to watch. This was the day Ashton's character was supposed to get a big kiss from his girlfriend, played by the actress Piper Perabo. In an attempt to cut any tension on the set, Perabo walked up to Demi and introduced herself. "Hi! You're gorgeous," she said. "I'll be kissing your boyfriend in ten minutes." Demi was amused.

The ice had been broken, and the kiss went off without incident. Into October, Ashton's professional life continued to take second place to the latest adventures in his romance with Demi. It was then that Ashton made a fateful decision.

He decided to take the love of his life home to meet Mom.

Ashton had maintained a fondness for the University of Iowa and its football team, the Hawkeyes. When he got wind of the upcoming homecoming game between the Hawkeyes and the University of Michigan, he thought it would be great to take Demi back for the game and have her meet his family. Demi, who had long before put down roots in Idaho, thought it would be fun to get back to a more laid-back climate for a few days.

More important, Ashton had always made a point of bringing the women he truly cared about home to meet his mother. It was an old-world trait that the wild life in the spotlight had failed to drive out of him. It also may have cut to the heart of Ashton's closeness to his family and especially his mother.

"I guess it's kind of Freudian," he once said with regard to his relationships with women. "But I really believe that every man wants a woman who's like his mother."

Freudian or not, it was important to Ashton that Diane like Demi.

The couple did their best to keep the trip hush-hush, but, as often happens, by the time Ashton's plane touched down in Iowa, paparazzi were already setting up camp outside his mother's door. Ashton really wanted to see the game, but with the press overrunning the town of Homestead and dogging their every step, they decided to cancel their game plans and instead just hang around his mother's house and spend time with his family.

Those plans were scuttled to a degree by the paparazzi's insistence on staking out the Portwood property, hoping for a chance shot of the happy couple.

"They parked up the road and walked down, back and forth, trying to get a glimpse of them," Ashton's mother told a local paper.

Diane during their visit also let it be known that Ashton, despite his rising fame, had made regular visits back home, often in disguise, wearing a wool cap and dark glasses. That statement ultimately served to increase the presence of paparazzi in their town to nearly year-round.

On their visit Ashton and Demi rode four-wheel-drive vehicles through the nearby fields and visited his brother, sister, and mother and stepfather. Diane was the guardian at the gate to the ever-encroaching press.

"When the paparazzi came to the door, I told them I'd call the law on them if they didn't leave. And when they didn't, that's what I did." No one was arrested and they continued to hang around.

Still, Demi and Diane talked for hours, and Ashton's mother came to the conclusion that despite her celebrity she was a real person. "We sat and talked about her kids and my kids and just had a great time."

Not long after their visit, Diane Portwood added her own theory about the future plans of her son and his actress girlfriend.

"Demi and Ashton are a great couple who are serious about their relationship," she said in an interview. "But they're going to wait at least another six months before marrying. When they were visiting, Ashton told his brother, Michael, not to rush into a marriage he was planning, so I know Ashton is going to take his own advice."

Diane also later acknowledged that she herself was married to a man eleven years younger than she. "If it's good enough for me, there's no reason why it shouldn't be good enough for my son."

Ashton and Demi's visit to Homestead was also an interesting case study in how small-town America reacts when one of their own becomes a celebrity. While he still took some good-natured ribbing on his visits home, the town of Homestead had finally come to embrace him as their own. And so while locals were initially willing to talk to reporters about their hometown hero, the onslaught of media interest later caused the townsfolk to circle their wagons. They were quick to call the law when a visiting reporter or paparazzo got too inquisitive; occasionally, they would take the matter into their own hands.

Such an incident took place during the summer of 2003 when a reporter for the *Los Angeles Times* came to town and asked the locals questions about Ashton. At one point in his investigation, the reporter was sitting in a bar when the telephone rang. It was Diane, complaining about the intrusion into their privacy. Taking his cue from Ashton's mother, the formerly friendly bartender flew into a rage, grabbed the reporter's notebook, threw it across the bar, led him to the entrance, and indelicately told him to get out of town.

The visit to Homestead immediately fanned the flames of speculation on where the relationship was going. Ashton, it was reasoned, had taken only girls that he was serious about to meet his mom, so in the eyes of the world this was serious business.

So was the round-the-clock work schedule that Ashton was keeping throughout the remaining months of 2003. He was either attending to some last-minute details on *The But-*

terfly Effect (which still had no solid release date), continuing negotiations on *The Village,* working on *That '70s Show* or *Punk'd*'s upcoming second season. It was a hellish pace that many speculated would finally catch up with him. Sleep obviously was not on Ashton's agenda: When he was not working, he was usually with Demi at some hip nightspot, often at hours so late that Demi could not keep up.

On those nights when Ashton went out stag, he was always true to his lady love. One notable occasion was the night when Ashton and his buddies from *That '70s Show* partied at the famous Joseph's Café. The group was hanging out in the VIP section of the trendy hangout and were constantly hit on by a bevy of beautiful women. Ashton ignored the attention.

Another such situation presented itself in November when Ashton, Demi, and Danny and Wilmer from *That '70s Show* were whooping it up at the Canal Room in New York. Around 2 A.M. Demi decided that she had had enough and went home. Rather than go with her, Ashton, with his friends, continued the party at the hip club Cielo. From the moment they entered the club, every female eye in the place was on Ashton. Anybody who read a paper or watched television knew that Demi and he were an item. But when they saw him stag with his buddies, it immediately became a free-for-all, as the women gathered around him.

A young blonde came up to him and made it very plain that she was up for anything. In earlier years, Ashton would have taken the bait in a heartbeat. But he was being true to Demi, and so, though they stayed at Cielo's for some time, Ashton spent most of it saying thanks but no thanks to women who were lining up to offer themselves to him.

The marriage rumors continued to fly. In November, the

word hit the entertainment news that Ashton and Demi planned to get married on Valentine's Day at the Bellagio Hotel in Las Vegas. One story reported that Ashton had actually gotten down on one knee and proposed to Demi (who said yes). It was also reported that Demi's ex, Bruce, had been contacted and was agreeable to giving the bride away. It was one of those reports that nobody was willing either to confirm or deny, which succeeded only in ratcheting up the already fever-pitch interest in their romance.

Needless to say, the Demi Moore–Ashton Kutcher relationship had become a cottage industry for every radio and television talk-show host in the nation at a loss for something to talk about. When Ashton appeared as a guest on the *Tonight Show,* Jay Leno grilled him mercilessly on the relationship. But in what turned into a wildly entertaining exchange, Ashton deftly sidestepped the questions about his relationship and turned them back on Leno, who is married to an older woman.

One morning, the radio host Rick Dees was feeding the audience the latest in laugh-inducing speculation on the Demi-Ashton wedding plans, when Demi unexpectedly called into the show and told Dees in no uncertain terms that the wedding story making the rounds "was completely made up."

Demi had been largely silent on the relationship, to the point of not even mentioning her young lover during a major magazine interview. But she was always being pressed on details, and occasionally a tiny bit would slip out. During an interview with the *Today Show* host, Matt Lauer, she said, "You should meet him. I think everybody's pretty excited when they meet him."

She also said in a BBC interview that the obsession with

Ashton and her relationship was totally out of control, with tabloid fables taking on a life of their own, such as the often heard on-again, off-again marriage plans. "I don't know what to think about it," she said. "I just try to keep going with the flow and stay out of the bull's-eye."

Easily the most defining moment in the couple's battle with the media over their privacy was the night Demi was a guest on *Late Night with David Letterman*. Letterman grilled Demi on the relationship with Ashton and the actress did her best to stay civil. Then she paused in the conversation and announced that she had just received a phone message from Ashton, who wanted to know when Letterman was going to marry the mother of his newborn child. Letterman's demeanor immediately changed. It was clear as he shrank back into his chair that he did not like the shoe being on the other foot.

Perhaps tiring of the constant media scrutiny, the couple would occasionally throw the press a loop by not appearing together in public. At that year's Teen Choice Awards, Ashton did show up but with Demi's child Scout. He walked off with five of the show's top honors. For a birthday party thrown by Kate Hudson for her rocker husband Chris Robinson, Ashton again showed up, this time with Demi's fifteen-year-old daughter, Rumer. The entire family unit, including Demi, was once again together and smiling for the cameras at the premiere of *Cheaper by the Dozen*.

Cheaper by the Dozen opened in December, and while the reviews were decidedly mixed, the film ended up doing well. More than one critic speculated that the opportunity of seeing Ashton in only a couple of scenes may have accounted for much of the film's strong opening weekend. Ashton was just happy to see another film in theaters.

By December, Ashton was working so hard on so many projects that he often could not keep them straight in his own head. He met with his management team, and they agreed that something had to go.

On December 12, Ashton announced that the second season of *Punk'd* would be the last. "We have had an incredible time doing the show," he said in a prepared statement, "and have decided, in the old Hollywood adage, to leave them wanting more."

That was the statement for public consumption. Reading between the lines, the cancelation of *Punk'd* seemed like nothing more than a good business decision. The show had painted Ashton into a corner as the on-camera jokester; the real reasons were that Ashton had gotten into producing and other things and that he wanted to be taken more seriously.

The reality was also that *Punk'd* and other aspects of his public image were unraveling.

Chapter Seven

Backlash

*P*unk'd had never been an easy show to produce, and Ashton, even before announcing that season two would be the last, often talked about the challenges.

To be successful, *Punk'd* always had to dance on the edge of courting extreme responses from its victims. Audiences were too sophisticated to deal with the tame responses of the victims of *Candid Camera*. This was the MTV generation. They wanted aggression, anger, and, yes, a degree of violence. They wanted somebody to mouth obscenities, raise a middle finger, and charge the camera crew. Anything less and audiences would have tuned out in droves. Ashton was pushing the envelope with *Punk'd,* and it was risky.

His initial camera crew had to be fired halfway through season one because it had become so recognizable that potential victims saw them coming, which immediately destroyed the gag. Once Ashton used up his circle of celebrity friends as *Punk'd* victims, he had to venture out into uncertain celebrity waters for his targets.

That's where the real trouble began.

It became evident, especially in the early stages of season two, that some celebrities did not have a sense of humor and that Ashton's *Punk'd* antics were more frequently resulting in a violent response. The rapper Missy Elliott became so enraged when she thought a diamond-encrusted cross she brought to a jewelry store to be cleaned had been lost, she completely lost her cool and was well on her way to destroying a glass jewelry case when Ashton rushed out of hiding and into camera range to stop her. In another incident, the bad-boy rocker Tommy Lee became so upset with the prank that he threatened to beat up the *Punk'd* camera crew. A first-season *Punk'd* episode with Carmen Electra and her musician husband, Dave Navarro, apparently got so ugly that it has never been aired.

"Some people have gotten pretty upset," Ashton admitted.

Volatile subjects may have been only the tip of the iceberg. Lurking below the surface of his celebrity jokes was the possibility of something worse.

During the second season a plan was hatched to prank a certain notorious white rapper (whom Ashton has refused to name). According to rumors, it was going to be the granddaddy of all *Punk'd* pranks, one designed to send the victim right over the edge. Unfortunately, the plan leaked and made its way back to the rapper, who was not pleased.

"We actually got a death threat called into the show's talent producer," said Ashton. "I don't want to name any names, but he was a white rapper, and it would have been a hell of a way to wind up on his next album."

While a lot of Ashton's celebrity peers were initially amused at the *Punk'd* antics, many now came out against the show. Alyssa Milano, then Justin Timberlake's girlfriend, said that Justin had been extremely upset at the prank Ashton did to him and that she would have warned him if she had known.

A prank that never even happened got Leonardo DiCaprio all hot and bothered. It seems that Ashton had plans to prank his supermodel girlfriend, Gisele Bündchen, by coating her house with plastic. DiCaprio got wind of it and was so angry that Ashton decided to cancel it. DiCaprio said, "Don't get me wrong. I watch the show all the time. But I just wouldn't want anyone near me involved." Bündchen, in a surprising bit of candor, said that his anger went much deeper than the prank. "Leo's so jealous of him," she said. "Leo just doesn't like him because he's so cute."

Bündchen's comment seems to have cut to the heart of the problem that celebrities and noncelebrities alike were starting to have with Ashton: jealousy. Ashton, barely twenty-five-years-old, seemed to have everything. Good looks, celebrity, loads of money, hot women. The package that was Ashton Kutcher just seemed too perfect, so perfect that even celebrities whose careers were further along than Ashton's felt threatened. Quite simply, Ashton was living too good a life, one that had other celebrities looking for any excuse to take him down a peg. So whether the barbs that were now coming Ashton's way were justified or not, human nature being what it is, they were to be expected.

Which all came as a shock to Ashton. He had always had a live-and-let-live attitude that precluded jealousy. He was happy that all his friends were successful. That anybody he knew wished him likewise bewildered and also saddened him.

Ashton was already well known for burning the candle at both ends, and while he continued to juggle everything thrown his way, by mid-2003 the word was that his workaholic nature was starting to get in the way of more mature projects, a case in point being the opportunity he was afforded to join the cast of Cameron Crowe's *Elizabethtown.*

Crowe had long been a filmmaker idol of Ashton's, so he was thrilled when the director asked him to read for him and discuss the character he would be playing in this high-profile drama. Reports indicated that the pair had agreed in principle to work together. Then things seemed to change.

According to news reports, Ashton, despite the film's changing schedules several times, had not been able to find time to do the film, so he had to decline. That was one reason.

Then there was the question that had dogged Ashton since he got into the business. Could he act well enough to do more mature roles that required more of him than lowbrow sitcom comedy flash? Unfortunately for Ashton, as late as 2003, the jury was still out. His erratic film record, in particular *My Boss's Daughter,* still followed him; as did the fact that his biggest film hits, *Dude, Where's My Car?* and *Just Married,* did not require much more of Ashton's talents than did playing Kelso on *That '70s Show.* It did not help that *The Butterfly Effect,* the film he considered as containing the best acting of his career, had once again been pushed back and was now slated for a late January 2004 release.

Not long after the scheduling conflict on *Elizabethtown*

story surfaced, a second story hit the entertainment press that touched on that very theory.

According to the report, Cameron Crowe was unhappy with Ashton's auditon read-throughs, each one allegedly being worse than the preceding one. The story also reported that it was not a scheduling conflict, as had been reported; that Crowe had in fact postponed the production because he had hoped that Ashton's read-throughs would get better. The story went on to say that when the director had all but given up, he suggested to Ashton that he take acting lessons.

Upon further examination, this theory seems to hold water. What actor in his right mind would not rearrange his schedule to be able to fit in a potential career-making role in a Cameron Crowe film? Cynics felt that if Ashton's acting skills had been called into question, a scheduling conflict would seem like a good face-saving move on his part.

Ashton did not sit silently by as his skills as an actor were called into question. In a recent interview, Ashton explained that his acting was not the problem. He claimed that he did actually have the role and had gone so far as to preshoot several episodes of *That '70s Show* so that he would be available to shoot the film. But when Crowe rescheduled the start of filming, Ashton was put in the position of either taking the role and compromising an entire shooting schedule for *That '70s Show* or walking away from the film. He chose the latter, stating that it would have been "virtually impossible" to do both.

Ashton's relationship with Demi, which had to this point been more a point of curiosity than anything else, also took some nasty hits in the press. Several stories reported that since relocating to Los Angeles, Demi had taken to showing up on the set of *That '70s Show* and watching him work. This was allegedly creating tension among the show's actresses and female crew members, who reported to certain tabloid outlets that Demi would often glare at them if they so much as smiled at her guy.

The actress Shannon Elizabeth, who had joined the show as Mike Kelso's love interest, had a particularly uneasy feeling about Demi's being on set all the time.

"I felt that if she was around, I might have to ask for permission," she said in an interview. And although the comment was perhaps in jest, the press was quick to run it in the most negative way possible.

And, in what has become a time-honored tradition of the tabloid press's building somebody up only to tear him or her down, outrageous tales of the couple appeared in print. One contended that Ashton and Demi had been fighting a lot in recent weeks, the cause being the alleged insane pressure Ashton was putting on Demi to get married. The story further speculated that the reason Ashton was in such a big rush was that he knew his sudden high profile had everything to do with their relationship and that he feared his career would go into a decline if they did not get married. Another story alleged that Ashton was uncomfortable with Demi's cordial relationship with her ex-husband, Bruce Willis, and that he was pressuring her to stop seeing him so often.

Ashton of course denied those accusations and contemplated legal action against the publishers of the more outrageous reports. But what Ashton failed to realize was that a lot of his current discomfort was of his own making.

From the beginning, he actively courted the press and took every opportunity to get his face in front of a camera, never stopping to realize that the entertainment media was not his friend and that the only thing he could count on was that they would eventually turn on him. Consequently, he began to be more tentative in public situations, which only led to further damaging reports.

One story making the rounds at this time had the normally friendly Ashton brushing off the request of a fan to take his picture. In another, he allegedly flew into a rage when somebody had taken a good-natured jab at the clothes he was wearing.

Friends also became a bit of a sore point for the young actor. While the core group that he met early in his Hollywood career and his buddies from *That '70s Show* had remained loyal and supportive, he heard rumblings from many of his so-called friends that he had deserted them for a glitzier Hollywood crowd that included the likes of Demi Moore and P. Diddy. Ashton categorically denied that he had traded in old friends for a flashier model, but he had to admit that he traveled in different circles these days.

Ashton was particularly unhappy at the idea that people were upset that he was hanging out with a black rapper. "If I was hanging out with a white guy who was on a TV sitcom, nobody would have a problem with that. But because I'm hanging out with P. Diddy and he's black, it's a big deal."

Ashton threw up his hands at the notion that he had gone Hollywood and at the sudden rush of nasty press. "People are afraid of what they don't understand, and they don't understand me."

What Hollywood did not understand about Ashton was that he did not fit into their preconceived notion of what an actor should be.

The serious filmmaking community tended to look at Ashton with a jaundiced eye. To many he was just a pretty-faced former runway model with limited acting skills who had gotten lucky. But Steven Soderbergh, the director of such films as *Traffic* and *Ocean's Eleven,* saw potential in the young man for a number of projects he had in the works. He got word to Ashton that he would be interested in having him audition.

For it, Soderbergh had Ashton read from a script from the cable-television series *K Street.* It was an audition that required the actor to show off his dramatic abilities, and Ashton, according to reports, performed well. The director was happy with Ashton's test and instantly envisioned him as the young love interest in one of as many as six projects that were in varying degrees of development. However, he had one reservation.

Soderbergh was a purist. To him, filmmaking was an art, and all of those who participated had to be serious artists. Consequently, he had a problem with actors who were too often in the spotlight, feeling that too much exposure took away from their craft. So he promised Ashton work at a future date if, according to reports, "he could remain up to par professionally." Soderbergh allegedly told the actor in no uncertain terms that if he saw him on the cover of one more magazine or photographed at one more party, he would be off his acting roster for any future pictures.

Ashton saw this as a major opportunity, and although his initial inclination was to continue to be a publicity hound, he began to shy away from his usual round of Hollywood parties and any place a photographer might be present. For a while it seemed to work. While hardly out of mind, he was rarely in sight.

But in October 2003, the second season of *Punk'd* was on the horizon, and Ashton could not very well avoid publicizing his own show. So he went out on the press circuit once again and hoped that Soderbergh would understand.

He did not, and the actor and director soon broke off their talks.

Ashton's role in *The Village* may or may not have fallen victim to his party-boy label. Press reports had gone quickly from saying that he was definitely in the film to saying that he was not in the film and never had been. Had image and alleged lack of skill cost Ashton another shot at the big time? Nobody would say for certain.

Ashton had long ago become polished in deflecting barbs directed at his perceived lack of acting skills, but in doing so, he often succeeded in making the case for his attackers, as witness this defense shortly after the success of *That '70s Show* and *Dude, Where's My Car?* The press had declared him the poster boy for dumb and dumber, and Ashton was doing his best to defend himself.

"You can become a star in a lot of ways," he has said. "You can be a great actor, which is the ideal way. Or you can be a terrible actor and make all the right choices. And there are people who are terrible actors making lots of money."

Critics jumped on him, using his own words to hang him out to dry, citing the quote and others like it as proof positive that Ashton was getting by solely on good looks and woefully marginal talent.

For Ashton, the free ride seemed over. After being Hollywood's fair-haired boy, the barrage of bad press, whether true or tabloid, over the past few months had brought him crashing back to reality. He was happy with his life both personally and professionally, but he realized that with celebrity came the slings and arrows. He was not about to change his ways, but he was going to be more vigilant about protecting his image.

Ashton was quick to threaten legal action when a publication in England made up a quote that made him sound like a low-life cretin. He was also quick to correct out-of-context quotes and old interviews that were recycled in a new context. Ashton had to agree up to a point that the press had treated him fairly. But with the onset of celebrity and his relationship with Demi Moore, the press suddenly turned on him in an almost spiteful way. While there was nothing he could do about all the lies and misrepresentations, he now spent an inordinate amount of his daily life correcting these falsehoods. To Ashton it all seemed so unnecessary.

Still, the body blows continued.

Hollywood was aflutter with the news that Ashton and Demi were planning on doing a remake of *The Graduate,* with Demi as the notorious Mrs. Robinson and Ashton as Benjamin Braddick. People were all over the life-versus-art angle and the rumor that after they secretly did a screen test that made the rounds, several studios were interested in the project.

But the slap in the face for Ashton was not far behind.

A story surfaced not much later that reported that Demi's production company had allegedly bought up the film rights to the Barbie and Ken dolls and was planning on producing a live-action movie. The story went on to say that while nobody was under consideration for the role of Barbie, Demi already had an actor in mind for the role of Ken.

It was Ethan Hawke. Ashton Kutcher not up to playing a Ken doll? It was funny, but to Ashton it was humiliating. The reality was that both Ethan and Ashton were being considered for roles in the film. But for Ashton's reputation, it was too late: The damage had been done.

The toughest thing to overcome was Ashton's sudden loss of freedom and privacy. Growing up in Iowa, he read the fan magazines, saw the pictures of the celebrities, and realized that, yes, these people were being photographed wherever they went. At that point it seemed like a cool thing. Now he knew the truth.

Many's the morning that Ashton got up to find an army of SUVs parked at the end of his driveway, paparazzi inside, waiting for him to leave. They would tail him to wherever he was going and snap away the first time he showed his face. Ashton knew that once he had gained a certain degree of celebrity his life was no longer his own, but that did not mean that he had to like it.

"I'm tired of seeing me. I think being chased, followed, and stalked by photographers is an obstacle."

Chapter Eight

The Future Is Now

Ashton spent the 2003 holiday season with Demi and the children. Christmas was full of holiday cheer and whimsy. Ashton reportedly presented Demi with a $17,000 tennis bracelet. Demi, who has always kept a humorous attitude toward the public's fascination with their age difference, filled Ashton's stocking with DVDs of her earlier films like *St. Elmo's Fire* and *About Last Night . . .* with a note saying he had been too young to watch them when they came out in the eighties. Also on Ashton's gift list was a DVD of *The Graduate,* an unsubtle aside to the larger-than-life fantasy they were presenting to the public.

New Year's was unbelievable. In an attempt to shake the

paparazzi, Ashton, Demi, and her children slipped off to the Parrot Cay resort in the Caribbean for a two-week holiday. There the couple rang in the New Year watching fireworks arc across the night sky and toasted 2004 with many cocktails.

"I got to spend two weeks with a wonderful, loving family," reflected Ashton. "It was the greatest gift I could get."

Ashton and Demi were as far away from the paparazzi as they could possibly get. In the midst of this idyllic island paradise, their feelings toward each other could do nothing but intensify. Amid the tropical splendor, the couple seemed the perfect picture of love in bloom. And to their way of thinking, nothing was going to break them up.

However, in the early part of January 2004, the sightings of everybody's favorite couple were less frequent. That both had professional lives to lead might have had something to do with it, but as always, gossip seemed the easier game to play. It led to speculation that they had broken up, had secretly gotten married and were on an extended honeymoon, or that they were secretly seeing other people.

Still others weighed in on the topic by saying that the whole Demi-Ashton fling had been the publicity stunt many had believed from the beginning and that the prank was now over. The more serious side of the press corps continued to bemoan the lack of anything serious in so many people's lives that made the thrill of following this celebrity love match such a big deal in the first place.

In an early January television interview, Ashton attempted once again to stem the mania for Demi and his relationship when he offered that the couple were in no great rush to the altar.

"Marriage [to Demi] isn't on the horizon soon. I don't

have any plans for it. I can check the datebook, but last I looked there wasn't anything in there on that."

This comment did much to fuel the notion that the whole Demi-Ashton relationship had been a farce. If in fact Ashton had hooked up with Demi to raise his professional profile, it seemed to have worked.

For while his film record continued to be erratic at best, studios knew a hot public property when they saw one, and so were lining up to offer him plum roles in a variety of higher-profile films. He had long been in negotiations with the comic Bernie Mac to do a comedy take on *Guess Who's Coming to Dinner*, tentatively titled *The Dinner Party*. In it, Mac would play the father who had to deal with his daughter's being in love with a white boy. The film was now a go and was tentatively scheduled to go into production in the spring of 2004. Also close to becoming a reality for Ashton was the long-anticipated movie version of the television chestnut, a long-held guilty pleasure of Ashton's, *The Dukes of Hazzard* in which Ashton and Paul Walker would reportedly play the Duke brothers while Britney Spears was seriously being considered for the role of Daisy.

Also on tap was a buddy cop movie called *The Regulators,* a *Lethal Weapon*–style action movie, and a romantic tale called *A Lot like Love*. Ashton was also being strongly considered for the all-star caper sequel *Ocean's Twelve,* which would reportedly once again feature George Clooney and Julia Roberts, and a remake of the classic children's fantasy *Charlie and the Chocolate Factory*.

Ashton also continued to flex his entrepreneurial muscles in the restaurant business when, with his buddies from *That '70s Show,* he once again took the plunge, this time investing in a West Hollywood sushi restaurant. As with his previous restaurant venture, Ashton was looking for a place to hang out and eat. And as with his first investment, the sushi restaurant showed an immediate profit.

There was even word that Ashton had finally agreed to do the long-anticipated sequel to *Dude, Where's My Car?*, *Seriously Dude, Where's My Car?*, although Ashton continued to jokingly insist that any *Dude* sequel would be a big-budget extravaganza with major stars doing cameos. Also on tap was a reunion between Ashton and Shawn Levy, the director of *Just Married*, in a football drama called *Overtime* about a college quarterback who spends time with his estranged father, also a quarterback, in the rough-and-tumble world of professional football. Ashton would also serve as executive producer on the movie. Based on the good relationship they had on *The Butterfly Effect*, Ashton, Bress, and Gruber put their heads together and came up with the idea for a one-hour drama about college life called *The House*. Ashton would be the executive producer, with an eye toward bringing the show to Fox.

Talk turned to the possibility of Ashton going from in front of the camera to behind it to direct his own film. He liked the idea but would tell anyone who would listen that he would not attempt directing until he could also do the jobs of everyone else on the set.

While the offerings remained primarily comedies, Ashton was grateful for the odd dramatic offers and was encouraged that he might finally shed the albatross that was Mike Kelso.

Uppermost in Ashton's mind at the moment was *The Butterfly Effect*, which late in 2003 had its release date confirmed for January 23, 2004. Ashton threw himself into the promotion for the film with a series of press interviews in Los Angeles. And although he had done countless interviews, the constant media pressure about his relationship with Demi made him uneasy about just sitting down and answering questions from a group of journalists with tape recorders rolling.

He hoped the reporters would focus on the movie and his acting. So did the publicists from New Line Cinema, who would have his costar, Amy Smart, sit in with him in many of the interview sessions in the hopes that the questions would not be solely directed at him. But he knew in his gut that most of the attention would be coming his way and that most of the questions would be about his relationship with Demi. Short of doing no press for the film, there was no way to avoid the personal questions.

His uneasiness was evident. Interviewers were quick to note that Ashton was tense and nervous during that early round of interviews. His usual smooth conversational style was forced and uncomfortable. He constantly clenched and unclenched his hands. When nobody objected, he would smoke. When the questions did come about his relationship, he tried to sidestep them with humorous comebacks but, more often than not, his discomfort with talking about his personal life was evident, as was his growing annoyance with being under a microscope.

"If you thought that everything you did or said on a daily basis could become public knowledge, you wouldn't do or say a lot of things," he said during one of those interviews.

When he was not being assaulted with personal questions, Ashton was more at ease. The impression interviewers got was that he was sincerely proud of his first dark dramatic role and that he was looking for this film to break him out of the *That '70s Show* image and into more challenging projects.

Although he would not admit it during interviews, it was apparent that a lot more was riding on *The Butterfly Effect* in terms of substantial future career plans for Ashton. Industry

observers had noted that he had really had only two legitimate movie hits and that even those did not show staggering
acting talent on his part. They also felt that his much publi-
cized love affairs caused him to be considered less a real actor
and more a publicity-seeking party guy with no real creative
ambitions.

The consensus around Hollywood was if *The Butterfly Effect* were a smash and his acting was up to par, very real opportunities might open up for the young actor. If not, Ashton
might well have only a truncated career that would mimic the
recent misfortunes of Freddie Prinze Jr., who started out like
a house on fire only to stumble into mediocrity and Scooby-
Doo movies.

Ashton did not seem concerned by the speculation about
how much hinged on the success of *The Butterfly Effect.* "If I
fail and never do another movie again, I've already done it. So
if I fail, that's all right."

Press coverage in general, even with the incessant intrusions into his personal life, also took a turn. To be sure, the
teen magazines and tabloids remained the major source of details on Ashton, usually focusing on Demi and his personal
life at the expense of his serious pursuits as an actor and producer. But deeper, more ambitious think pieces centering on
how celebrities come into being and how Ashton was seemingly succeeding by not playing the usual games hit the
stands in hipper, upscale magazines like *Details* and *GQ.* The
tone of the stories was less flip and condescending, and the
questions posed by serious journalists brought out the more
enlightened, thoughtful side of Ashton.

In many quarters Ashton continued to remain the butt of
bad jokes about his acting talent and personal life. But the press
was slowly coming around to giving him grudging respect.

With this new round of stories, a different side of Ashton Kutcher began to emerge.

Missing from many of these stories was the notion that Ashton Kutcher was a dumb model who had gotten very lucky. Ashton was now being perceived as being business-savvy in a street sort of way. While he was pictured as somebody relying more on gut reaction and hunches, his management team was very much of the old school in guiding his career and dealing with the media. When a story or an interview did not suit their client's purpose, they put pressure on the publication to turn things their way.

This was much in evidence in late 2003 when the *Los Angeles Times* was set to run a massive feature on Ashton's hometown and career. Ashton and his publicists had no problem with the story, just with the timing of its release. The story was slated for an August 2003 publication; Ashton and his team preferred that the story run in January to help promote the release of *The Butterfly Effect.*

When the *Times* refused to hold the piece, Ashton refused to be interviewed. The same thing happened when *Details* announced that Ashton would be their September 2003 cover boy, a move that reportedly necessitated the last-minute removal of Rob Lowe from that spot. But when Ashton and his team discovered that the tone of the piece would be more of how Hollywood creates its stars, such as Ashton, and would be cynical, he refused to participate.

"We're very clear on what Ashton will and will not do," his partner Goldberg declared. "This way we've been able to control his career."

Ashton's worldwide celebrity continued to have an effect on his hometown of Homestead. By now his regular comings and goings there had become common knowledge, and it seemed that reporters had taken up permanent residence there, even when Ashton was nowhere to be seen.

"Every week I get a call," said McDonald, the high school principal. "If anybody is getting a little fed up about it, it's his folks and myself. I've had MTV, VH1, and *Entertainment Tonight* march right through the front doors of the school. I had a group of journalists from London just walk right in with their cameras. It's gotten to the point where it's like, 'Hey guys, we're trying to run an education system here.' And these interviews can take a long time. A lot of time they'll come in here at ten in the morning and still be here at five in the afternoon.

"I still think, by and large, the community is very proud and excited for Ashton. The kids are still pumped up about him. They all want to lay claim and say he's my second cousin, thrice-removed. Everybody wants to have a piece of him."

In early 2004, Ashton's Katalyst Productions announced that it had closed a deal with MTV for another show, called *My New Best Friend*. Based loosely on a British series of the same name, *My New Best Friend* offers contestants a substantial cash prize if they can convince friends or family that they have never met before. Ashton was set to produce the series but would not appear on camera.

As if Ashton's meteoric rise needed any further validation, the motion picture exhibitors named him the male star of tomorrow in their year-end poll. The award goes annually to the actor the exhibitors feel will be a top moneymaker for years to come. On the surface merely another award to add to his growing list of popularity honors, this award meant a lot more to the longevity of his career. It meant that the all-important exhibitors would continue to book his films into theaters and for longer runs. It also meant that they and his fans paid no attention to the critics who seemed to have made it a personal crusade to trash his work.

That '70s Show continued to be the cornerstone of his career, and one that fed into the ongoing speculation on what made him such a top draw despite a mediocre movie record. The show, as of mid-January, was mired at number sixty in the all-important Nielsen television ratings. The reality was that the show had never been what one would call a ratings winner; unlike such Fox shows as *The X-Files* and *The Simpsons*, it had never gotten close to the top twenty. Yet largely on the strength of Ashton's talent and bigger-than-life persona, it was a show that was always on viewers' minds, one that Fox felt was worth keeping around.

What kept Ashton tied to the show went a lot deeper than mere ratings, for while his career had long before eclipsed that of his fellow cast members, he still maintained that *That '70s Show* was his rock and the place he went to for support and security. Which was why, despite his hectic schedule, he was there with the rest of his cast early in January for an interview session at the annual television critics get-together in Los Angeles, where he stood tall for team unity.

"I think we're a team," he told the assembled reporters. "I think what we enjoy doing together is making this show, and we enjoy making other people laugh at our work."

Ashton also conceded at that session that his life had changed for him over the past few months and that he had experienced personal scrutiny unlike any he could ever have imagined. "The last couple of months have been a little different, and that makes this time working on the show even more valuable. I'm not alone now. I have no alone time. So when I get to the set, it really is like a breather."

At this interview the cast members collectively agreed that the 2005 season of *That '70s Show* would most likely be the last. The timing for that announcement seemed right. The show had had a long run, and the entire cast was already moving onto bigger and better things. Sometime after May 2005 Ashton would be free of the weekly television grind.

Ashton's relationship with Demi Moore through the early part of January had also cooled in the public's perception. They were still occasionally spotted out and about. Around Christmas time, one enterprising paparazzo caught some video footage of Ashton and Demi racing through an airport. Entertainment pundits stepped in with the theory that Ashton and Demi were tired of the endless exposure so, perhaps fearing the backlash that everyone had been predicting, had decided to keep their relationship under cover for a while. There was also the theory that in the public's mind the May-December relationship had finally run its course and nobody was interested anymore.

If that were the case, Ashton would be happy.

"Do I rejoice in the fact that I cannot leave my house without being followed?" he said in response to the incessant press coverage of his romance. "No, it's a little creepy. But I wouldn't have it go away because if it went away, I wouldn't be in the position I'm in right now."

New Line Cinema had carefully trotted out its press campaign for *The Butterfly Effect*. There had been a handful of sneak previews of *The Butterfly Effect* for the press, and the word of mouth was very good. Ashton felt that the true test of the film would be when it had its official unveiling at the Sundance Film Festival, a week before its scheduled release. So it was with a mixture of excitement and nervousness that Ashton traveled to Park City, Utah, for the prestigious film festival that every year brought out a mixture of established superstars and brash newcomers to see a nearly nonstop barrage of films of every conceivable type and to strike distribution deals with interested studios.

"I've never been to Sundance before," he said in a recent interview. "I always told myself I'm not going to go until I have a movie there. I didn't want to be there and be the guy hanging out. I'm looking forward to being a part of a very cool thing."

A very cool thing that included all sorts of swag offered by the local merchants and the Sundance organizers to its more famous attendees. Ashton was not one to turn down a freebie, so he was like a kid in a candy store as he drew up a list that included winter clothes, skis, boots, jackets, goggles, and gloves. When the plane touched down in Park City, he would quickly find himself dressed in the finest gear other people's money could buy.

Ashton did not feel self-conscious about using his name for gain. He had a long history of accepting stuff from people and, while he was not aggressive in pursuing free things, he rarely said no to an offer. He could justify it by the fact that by his wearing of these things, he was a walking billboard for the companies that made them. That it appeared self-centered and selfish to many did not bother him. It was all just another perk for all his hard work.

Against the backdrop of snow-capped mountains and in laid-back hip nightspots and eateries, Ashton soaked up the Sundance experience. When not doing interviews in support of his film, he schmoozed with his fellow professionals, wandered the streets, played hide-and-seek with the ravenous fans who had come to Park City on the off chance of meeting him, and took in the sights of the world famous city. At one point in the Sundance madness, Ashton sneaked off to the mountains and indulged himself in a bit of snowboarding.

Ashton had insisted that Demi accompany him to Sundance. He felt he needed her support, and, if the truth be known, he couldn't think of a more picturesque spot to spend some time with the woman he loved. With the onslaught of celebrities in Park City, including another new romantic couple, Paris Hilton and Nick Carter, they had hoped they would be able to occasionally lose themselves in the sheer numbers of people. But while they occasionally got off by themselves, it was next to impossible to completely avoid the paparazzi. But by then they were so hardened to the notion that they would have no privacy, they were able to ignore the cameras and just go about their business.

Their business led to the one minor tabloid tidbit during their stay. It was reported that Demi, with Ashton elsewhere, had met privately with her former boyfriend, Guy Oseary, at the hotel where she and Ashton were staying. While those in the know insisted that the meeting was all business, it was reported that the very public room where the pair met was cleared of all other people.

Ashton's media encounters ran the gamut from gossipy to serious, with, he noticed, an emphasis on the latter. For better or worse, Ashton's career had preceded him, so there was a large degree of curiosity among the serious film press who pressed him on creative rather than personal matters. Ashton was grateful for the change of pace, feeling for the first time that he was being taken seriously as an actor and producer. Of course, there were the expected tabloid questions about his personal life, but by this time Ashton found them easy to deflect or ignore.

Or make fun of. In one round of media interviews, it was

jokingly proposed that his and Demi's relationship had stolen the thunder of the similarly beaten-to-death romance between Ben Affleck and Jennifer Lopez. Ashton joked that he would have to kick Ben and Jennifer's act back into high gear so that they would once again have to deal with the heat. Unfortunately, in a matter of days it was announced that Ben and Jennifer had broken up, which left Ashton and Demi all alone in the paparazzi's crosshairs.

But while he could joke about it, he was often annoyed at the tabloid questions. It had gotten to the point where he expected the first question out of an interviewer's mouth to be about his relationship with Demi. Most of the time he just dealt with it. But he did lose his cool in the barrage of press interviews when one daring reporter suggested that the spike in his career was due to his ongoing relationship with Demi Moore.

"Let's just recap for a moment," he exploded. "Before I met her, I managed to figure out how to be on *That '70s Show*, I managed to produce my own TV show and managed to do a couple of films that did extremely well. I already had a pretty good career before I met my significant other, and I'll have a pretty good one after. I don't think it's all because of who I'm dating. I don't think that it's necessarily the different women that I've dated that have put me in the spotlight."

The age difference between Demi and himself continued to be of ongoing interest, and Ashton, in one interview, took offense at what he considered a not well veiled form of discrimination.

"I've dated older women. I've dated younger women. I don't go, 'Wow! This person is older than I am.' I don't put boundaries on myself based on age or race or anything. I don't discriminate."

At many press encounters, when the questions were about his movie, he would maintain that "*The Butterfly Effect* is really a twisted, different change of pace film for me. It focuses more on the mental anguish of a human."

In the days leading up to the opening of the festival, there were grumblings that the Sundance Festival, created to showcase unknown talents, had become saturated with big-star, big-studio films that already had major distribution deals. This year *The Butterfly Effect* took some prescreening criticism as a prime example of what the festival had become. Still, as the opening of the festival loomed closer, the buzz at Park City centered largely on *The Butterfly Effect*. It was a buzz that got people into the theater. Of course, once the film flickered across the screen, good or bad, all bets were off.

The night the film screened at Sundance, the actor was on pins and needles. He nervously toyed with his clothing before deciding that a white cowboy hat, kerchief, and a white shearling jacket would work for the premiere. One of the largest theaters at the festival, the Eccles, had been chosen. The buzz on the film had made *The Butterfly Effect*'s first screening hot, so its nearly 1,300 tickets were quickly gobbled up.

Ashton made his way to the theater, bypassing the expected crush of press waiting outside, and found his seat. Ten minutes later, Demi entered and sat down next to him. As expected the packed theater craned its collective heads when first Ashton and then Demi entered. The couple pretended not to notice as they waited for the lights to go down.

Ashton did get up to address the audience before the screening began. Noting that he was totally out of place in the parka-clad crowd, he quipped, "They told me this was Sundance and I had to dress up like Butch Cassidy and the Sundance Kid. Now I'm standing here like a jerk."

As the film played out, Ashton anxiously scanned the hall, listening for the slightest remark or titter that would indicate something had registered good or bad with the audience. The response was not encouraging. There were moments in the film when the audience laughed. When Ashton played a straight dramatic scene, there were audible chuckles from the audience. More than one major newspaper reported that the film was hooted off the screen.

Later that night, at a party given by New Line Cinema, Ashton was in a much more relaxed state of mind. Friends and strangers alike came up to him to tell him that they loved the movie. As he partied the night away, Ashton felt he had cleared an all-important hurdle: acceptance, even on a superficial level, by his peers. But the audience response to the screening had him concerned.

Ashton spent the next day as almost everybody else in America did: watching a National Football League conference championship game in a private Park City lounge with Demi and their good friends Courteney Cox and David Arquette. (For the record, Ashton was rooting for the Philadelphia Eagles, who lost.) But his mind was only partially on the game.

What he focused his thoughts on was January 23, the true test of *The Butterfly Effect* and, possibly, his career. In his heart, Ashton simply wanted to do good work and be recognized for his efforts. The frustration was that when it came to critical opinions, he did not feel he got a fair shake.

The first reviews of *The Butterfly Effect* would hit the internet and trade papers within twenty-four hours of the Sundance screening. They were mixed.

Variety dismissed the movie as "overcooked and somberly self important" while comparing Ashton's acting to what the reviewer perceived as the lackluster talents of Josh Hartnett.

The *Hollywood Reporter* provided this keeper. "Kutcher makes the incredible creditable by approaching each of his altered roles with realistic acting."

According to eFilmCritic.com, "Kutcher handles himself well in the role."

The online website Reel Views balanced the scales when it said, "While Kutcher doesn't embarrass himself, he is miscast. He lacks the gravitas necessary to pull off the part with complete conviction."

Ashton had long since resigned himself that critics were never going to love what he did. But when the first batch of particularly vicious reviews of *The Butterfly Effect* went public, he felt so beat up that he promptly canceled all remaining interviews except those he knew would be friendly. New Line Cinema confirmed that some interviews had in fact been canceled but because of scheduling, not because of the early reception to the film.

But people believe what they want to believe, and unfortunately, people seemed inclined to believe the worst. In their eyes, Ashton could not act, and nothing short of winning an Oscar would change their minds. The jealousy factor was very much a consideration when it came to judging anything done by Ashton.

Fortunately, Ashton did not have to spend the next six days idle or pondering the first mixed reviews. He returned to Los Angeles and work on *That '70s Show*. There were business meetings and future plans to finalize. At one point in late 2003, Katalyst Productions had reportedly come up with ideas for as many as half a dozen new television ideas that were being readied to be shopped to the networks. As in any brainstorming session, some ideas were better than others. But one thing remained certain. When Ashton's name was attached on any level, networks lined up to get the pitch.

There were also what he hoped would be the final round of television talk-show appearances to help sell *The Butterfly Effect*. It would be a nonstop crisscrossing of the United States in which he would appear with the usual suspects: Regis Philbin, Jay Leno, David Letterman. He would have to put up with yet another round of Demi comments, softball questions about the movie, and being the brunt of lame jokes about being a himbo. But Ashton had been this route before and felt comfortable.

Ashton was in such good spirits that he good-naturedly taunted the paparazzi that continued to hound him by showing up at different events in outrageous disguises. During a stint as an awards presenter in New York for the AOL Movie nominations, he gave the assembled photographers something to shoot when, after fielding the umpteenth question about Demi, he took off in a Groucho Marx duck walk around the room.

In the midst of the prerelease film hype, the specter of a Demi-Ashton marriage was once again raised by the tabloids in a story that announced that the couple would be getting married in May, that Bruce Willis would be in attendance, and that the couple were planning on having a baby in the near future.

Ashton's frustration on this topic had reached the point where he could only laugh and bemoan that the press continued to say that Demi and he were getting married.

And once again Ashton was faced with having to drop everything to deny the rumors. This time it was on his latest visit to *Late Night with David Letterman*. "We haven't talked about marriage. I'm not lining up at the altar."

In yet another interview some weeks later, he again stated that marriage was not in their future.

"It's so not true. There's no ring, no engagement, no wedding plans. But what we say doesn't mean anything. I've finally realized that the truth has nothing to do with what those people write."

Barring anything unforeseen, the long-anticipated *The Dinner Party* loomed on the horizon as his next feature, one that after the challenges of attempting to carry his first drama would no doubt be a welcome return to a much less stressful acting job.

Ashton now felt in a state of grace as he looked back on his life and career. A lot of observers speculated that *The Butterfly Effect*, with its heavy message and many spiritual and sociological elements, had caused Ashton to reexamine his life in other than material, black-and-white terms. The theory was also advanced that after years of driving hard in pursuit of success, Ashton had finally decided to slow down.

Part of Ashton's self-searching may be attributed to Demi's introducing him to the religion of kaballah. Ashton has not publicly talked about his religious preferences. Whether his philosophical side was the result of Demi's influence or some long dormant personal feelings coming through remains a question that Ashton has yet to explore publicly. But there are hints in his recent interviews that religion and inner peace are a big priority.

"I think that as human beings we're all really very complicated," he recently stated in a mixture of simple and complex philosophy. "It's important for me to be a good person, to do things that make me happy, and to do it for the sake of sharing it with others."

Whatever the reason behind such statements, it remained

that Ashton had turned philosophical about his success and said that if none of this had happened he would no doubt be attending MIT or Purdue at this point, getting his master's degree, and being quite happy in his choice.

"I'm always happiest when I'm doing something I like. And right now I'm very happy doing what I'm doing."

The Butterfly Effect opened on January 23. True to form, the reviews for both the film and Ashton were mixed, ranging from positive to constructively critical to downright vicious and nasty. Many critics took particular delight in putting down Ashton's acting talents.

Ashton had resigned himself to the attacks. "Some people are going to hate what I do no matter what I do."

But Ashton always felt that like his previous films, *The Butterfly Effect* was going to be critic-proof and would rise or fall on word of mouth and his already considerable fan base.

The early returns were encouraging. On its opening day, *The Butterfly Effect* brought in $6.2 million, a figure comparable to the opening day totals of Ashton's previous films. By Sunday night, it was official. *The Butterfly Effect* had earned $17.1 million to come in number one of the weekend box-office totals.

However, naysayers would not give him a break. Media observers insisted that curiosity over whether Ashton could actually act was the main reason the film had done so well. Ashton just threw up his hands. He was not going to catch a break in this life. His movie was number one, so he did not care.

Ashton turned down the pressure when he agreed to be a presenter at the annual Golden Globes ceremony. He was not feeling well but felt he could not pass up the opportunity. So midway through the show, dressed to the nines, he hit the stage to a thunderous applause, sharing light-hearted patter with his copresenter, the perpetually scowling Ice Cube. The producers of the show, looking to inject drama into Ashton's appearance, immediately cut to an audience shot of his ex, Brittany Murphy. To her credit, Murphy took the intrusion in good spirits.

Ashton had such a good time that when approached by a reporter backstage, he stopped to answer a couple of questions. Of course the first question out of the reporter's mouth was, "Is it true that Demi and you are getting married in May?" Ashton reportedly rolled his eyes. And then answered the question.

"The good news is that when we're not married in May, all those stories that have been written will be proven untrue. The bad news is that then the stories will say we're getting married at Christmas, and I'll have to spend the next six months denying those stories."

Ashton was feeling too sick to hit the parties afterward, so he went straight home and watched the Golden Globes ceremonies on tape in the comfort of his home. He was away from the questions and the paparazzi, and the silence seemed awfully good.

Not long after the opening of *The Butterfly Effect,* the tabloids and fan magazines were on fire with the reports that Ashton and Demi's main competition on the celebrity romance front, Ben Affleck and Jennifer Lopez, had called it quits. Ashton knew immediately that the media pressure on his relationship would increase a hundredfold. But he did not care, because he had more important things to think about. Like the announcement that the on again off again *Punk'd* was now officially on again, and that the production on a new season's worth of episodes would begin shortly.

Going into 2004, Ashton Kutcher was a legitimate star on both the big and small screen. His relationship with Demi Moore, rather than falling victim to rampant press scrutiny, appeared to be real and growing deeper, and the possibilities over the long haul for the two of them to live happily ever after were good. He had survived the slings and arrows of preconceived notions and the rabid Hollywood environment and emerged at the top of the Hollywood heap by sticking to his guns.

"I don't like to lose. I've always lived by the philosophy, 'Always be happy but never be satisified.' "

Ashton Kutcher celebrated his twenty-sixth birthday on February 7, 2004. By Hollywood standards, he had already lived a lifetime.

Ashton Kutcher On-Screen

Actor in Movies

Title	Year Released	Role
The Butterfly Effect	2004	Evan Treborn
Cheaper by the Dozen	2003	Hank (uncredited)
My Boss's Daughter	2003	Tom Stansfield
Just Married	2003	Tom Leezak
Texas Rangers	2001	George Durham
Dude, Where's My Car?	2000	Jesse Richmond
Down to You	2000	Jim Morrison
Coming Soon	1999	Louie
The Distance	1997	(No information available)

Actor in Television

Title	Year	Role
Grounded for Life	2002	Scott
Just Shoot Me	2001	Dean Cassidy
That '70s Show	1998–present	Mike Kelso

Producer

Title	Year	Function
The Butterfly Effect	2004	Executive Producer
Punk'd	2003	Producer
My Boss's Daughter	2003	Coproducer

Writer

Title	Year
Punk'd	2002–03

SOURCES

Interviews were conducted, with Tom McDonald and Larry Lockwood. Dave McDonnell was also integral in pointing me to useful information.

The following wire services, newspapers, and magazines proved excellent sources of information and anecdotes: *Flaunt, People, Los Angeles Times, InStyle,* the *Hollywood Reporter, New York Daily News, Us, GQ, TV Guide, Twist,* Associated Press, *Teen Movieline, New York Post, The Face, New York Times, Cedar Rapids Gazette, Paper* magazine, *British Cosmo, Seventeen, YM* magazine, *USA Today, Daily Star, Heat, Denver Post, Premiere, Teen Tribute, The Sun, San Francisco Chronicle, Cleveland Sun, Austin Chronicle, Cosmopolitan, New York* magazine, *Iowa City Press-Citizen, Interview, Starstruck, Chicago Sun-Times, Empire, Film Threat,* the *Village Voice, Pittsburgh Tribune-Review, Star, Des Moines Register, Salt Lake City Tribune, Variety, Washington Post, London Daily Mirror, The Star Phoenix, Toronto Sun,* Reuters, *Los Angeles Daily News, Cosmogirl, Orange County Register, Pasadena Star-News, San Francisco Examiner, Arizona Daily Star, Details, Rolling Stone.*

The following internet sites were helpful: First and always, thanks to Google News for keeping me up to date; also BBC Films, Cinemas Online, Buzzle.com, Entertainment News Wire, World Entertainment News Network, Scotsman.com, People Online, People Insider, Ashton Kutcher Network, Teen Hollywood.com, Bakersfield Channel.com, Miami.com, In

Review.com, Jam! Showbiz, E! Online, My Kida Space, MTV, ChannelOne.com, BBC Radio News, IMDB, Underground Online, Sci Fi Wire, Hollywood.com, ET, CTV, Zap2it, Film Stew, Box Office Prophets.

The following television programs and specials were also instrumental in piecing together the story: *Late Night with David Letterman,* the *Tonight Show with Jay Leno, The View, Driven,* CNN Live Today, CNN Sunday Morning.